EASY HAWAIIAN COOKBOOK

EASY
HAWAIIAN
COOKBOOK

70 Simple Recipes
for a Taste
of the Islands

CHEF PHILIP "IPPY" AIONA

ROCKRIDGE
PRESS

First Rockridge Press trade paperback edition 2022

Rockridge Press and the Rockridge Press logo are trademarks or registered trademarks of Callisto Media Inc. and/or its affiliates in the United States and other countries and may not be used without written permission.

For general information on our other products and services, please contact our Customer Care Department within the United States at (866) 744-2665, or outside the United States at (510) 253-0500.

Paperback ISBN: 978-1-63878-067-0 | eBook ISBN: 978-1-63878-279-7

Manufactured in the United States of America

Interior and Cover Designer: Lisa Schreiber
Art Producer: Sue Bischofberger
Editors: Annie Choi and Sierra Machado
Production Editor: Matthew Burnett
Production Manager: Martin Worthington

Photography © 2022 Hélène Dujardin, with food styling by Lisa Rovick, cover and pp. vi, vii-ix, x, 16, 34, 58, 70, 73, 84, 96, and 108; photography used under license from iStockphoto.com, pp. 4-5, 9, and 110; photography used under license from shutterstock.com, p. 8.

Illustrations used under license from iStockphoto.com.

Cover recipe: Poke Bowl, page 64

10 9 8 7 6 5 4 3 2 1

This book is dedicated to Mama Masayo,
who gave me my first Chinese cleaver,
inspiring me to become a chef and teaching
me the importance of loving what you do.

CONTENTS

INTRODUCTION

Aloha, my name is Philip Kahaku Aiona, but everyone just calls me Ippy. Before I tell you about myself, I first want to extend a warm *mahalo* (thank you) from my *ohana* (family) to you for reading this book. Whether you are here for nostalgia or strictly for the *ono* (tasty) grinds (food), I hope in some way that I can bring the beautiful islands of Hawai'i to your kitchen.

I was born and raised in the small *paniolo* (cowboy) country town of Waimea on the Big Island of Hawai'i. My dad is Hawaiian, Portuguese, and Chinese and was born in Hilo (also on the Big Island). My mom is an Italian American from New York who ventured across the continent and Pacific Ocean to Hawai'i for college, met a handsome Hawaiian, and had a family; the rest is Aiona history. When I was growing up, my dad had a Hawaiian plate lunch restaurant called the Kamuela Deli. Every day after school, I would walk to the restaurant with one of my friends (it wasn't hard to convince any of them), and we would have dinner. After dinner, their parents picked them up, and I would do my homework on one of the tables in the front with the old regulars until my dad closed for the night and drove us both home.

I have a very deep respect and connection with Hawaiian food. Most cookbooks are a collection of recipes, put together by chefs, bloggers, and home cooks through trial and

error. These are more than just recipes for me—this book is a collection of my past, present, and future.

I attended culinary school and have had a handful of businesses and projects, successes as well as failures. I currently own Ippy's Hawaiian BBQ—open since 2012—and we mostly use the original binder filled with the recipes from my dad's restaurant. These recipes are not supposed to be long and confusing (after all, this book is called the *Easy Hawaiian Cookbook* for a reason). This book is for the casual cook or anyone searching for that special meal to transport them back to the islands with each delicious, memory-inducing bite.

Hawaiian food was never meant to be complicated or fancy; it is food meant to bring people together, which is reflected in the culture. As far back as I can remember, whether it was New Year's at Grandma's in Kalapana or weekends at Uncle Scotty's in Keaukaha, everything revolved around family, food, and cold beers. Now that I'm a father of a beautiful two-year-old girl and have another one on the way, I know that my children will grow up spending their school nights at the restaurant, and Hawaiian food will be their present, future, and eventual past. Hawaiian food will always be a link through time tying us all together and binding us to our culture, family, and the islands that we all love and call Hawai'i. Allow this book to be your guide to create new wonderful memories with your ohana.

Hawaiian Teriyaki
Barbecue Beef
PAGE 40

CHAPTER ONE

Bringing Hawai`i Home

In this chapter, we will dive into the
wonderful world of Hawaiian cuisine—
from traditional Hawaiian food,
including canoe plants, to plate lunches—
and explore the amazing cultures
and people who brought those dishes
here. Hawai'i's diverse "melting pot" of
cultures has allowed our people to create
a unique and special cuisine that takes
the best of many worlds and turns them
into our own.

WHAT IS HAWAIIAN FOOD?

If we had to define what Hawaiian food is by putting it in a box, we would have two main categories. The first would be traditional Hawaiian food, which would include the canoe plants like taro, *'ulu* (breadfruit), *'uala* (sweet potato), *kava* (a soothing beverage that relaxes you), and *kukui* (candle nut), as well as some animals (pigs, chickens, and dogs) that the Polynesians first brought with them to the islands. You can find some of these foods at lū'aus, but you have a better shot of seeing traditional dishes like kalua pig, *hoio* (fern shoot) salad, poi (taro root dish), *kulolo* (taro and coconut dessert), and *pipikaula* (salted and semi-dried beef) at a local *pā'ina* (party).

The second category of Hawaiian food would be what we call "plate lunch" and is a conglomeration of the diverse cultures that moved to Hawai'i during the plantation era and meshed their foods together (see page 4). Having grown up in Hawai'i, I feel that I had an advantage over my classmates in culinary school. If you grow up in a Mexican home, chances are you grew up surrounded by Mexican food and its culture. If you grew up in an Italian home, it would be Italian, and so on. But if you grew up in a Hawaiian home, you were exposed to a diverse mix of influences like Chinese, Japanese, Korean, Filipino, Portuguese, and of course, Hawaiian cuisine. During a trip to a local restaurant, you have your choice of teriyaki, Korean fried chicken, *laulau* (meat, usually pork, wrapped in taro leaves and slow cooked), adobo, chicken katsu, and specialties from many cultures. I had an extra-large helping of this because I grew up in my dad's Hawaiian plate lunch restaurant, so I was exposed to every single step of the process. This book is your guide to cooking local plate lunch–style Hawaiian food the easy way.

A Note on Spelling

Keep an eye out for some of the words we use in this book. Hawaiians have our own way of saying lots of things, and this form of broken English is called "pidgin." Some ingredients may have different names, and I have provided these words throughout. There aren't many through the book, and I will always try to point it out when using pidgin terminology.

ONO MADE EASY

Creating the smooth and sticky paste Hawaiians call poi requires an *imu* (underground earth oven) and a poi pounder for pounding the *kalo* (taro). Making kalua pig also requires using an earth oven to cook the meat underground for hours. These things can seem intimidating to anyone who hasn't grown up cooking Hawaiian food. Well, I am here to tell you that Hawaiian food is not supposed to be intimidating. As a matter of fact, it is supposed to be quite the opposite: Hawaiian food is meant to be inclusive, simple, and delicious. Hawaiian food is cooking beef stew on a Sunday with your grandma or making laulau with your ohana for a graduation pā'ina. Hawaiian food is meant to bring people together.

This book is for anyone who wants to recreate the dishes from the islands that they love. I will help you discover the alternate ingredients and techniques needed to create these dishes wherever you are. Creating a dish like kalua pig with no earth oven is as simple as adding a dash of smoked salt and liquid hickory (found in most grocery stores). Utilizing the enzymes of a pureed pineapple will help cut down your cooking time for delicious pig *opu* (belly). With this book, you will have the confidence to cook memory-inducing meals from the islands, so you can bring the taste of aloha to you and your ohana with little fuss or stress.

BUILDING YOUR HAWAIIAN PANTRY

Open any pantry in a local Hawaiian household, and nine times out of ten you will find the same ingredients. Here are essential items to stock in your pantry:

Brown and granulated white sugar: C&H sugar (California and Hawai'i) is my favorite brand to use. If a recipe calls for brown sugar, try to use light brown sugar.

Canned meats: Canned meats, in particular Spam, are a staple in most Hawaiian homes. Other canned meats include Vienna sausage and corned beef.

Cornstarch: This will be key in many recipes throughout the book. I usually use Argo brand because it seems to be the most widely available. Keep in mind that not all cornstarch is created equally. Some require a little extra when adding to recipes.

Fish sauce: Patis or Lucky Brand fish sauce are widely available.

The Melting Pot of the Pacific

Plate lunch has become a staple for the people of Hawai'i, a way to identify who we have become and our different cultures. When sugar tariffs were eliminated on shipments to the mainland in the mid-1800s, Hawai'i's sugar industry began to rapidly expand. This single event created a ripple effect that is still being felt today. This catalyst caused hundreds of thousands of people to immigrate to Hawai'i to work on plantations, not only creating a whole new type of cuisine but also creating thousands of new families in the process.

I can say that without this event, I would not be here. My dad's ancestors were Hawaiian, Chinese, and Portuguese and traveled from Canton, China, and the Azores to these beautiful islands in the middle of the Pacific with hopes of plentiful work and extra money to send to their families back home. Chinese, Japanese, Korean, Portuguese, Hawaiian, and Filipino people made up the large sugarcane plantation

A TIMELINE OF CULTURAL INFLUENCES

300 to 500 / POLYNESIAN SETTLERS

Polynesian voyagers brought many plants with them, including taro, which they used to make poi. They also brought pigs, chickens, and dogs, as well as the original lū'au celebration— they would raise pigs and cook them in an underground oven for a feast to celebrate the birth of a child and many other occasions.

1778 to 1848 / BRITISH AND AMERICANS

The first Europeans who landed on the island of Kauai were Captain James Cook and his crew from the British Royal Navy, followed by the first US missionaries, who arrived in 1820.

1852 to 1887 / CHINESE

Though records exist of Chinese workers arriving as early as 1788, more than 50,000 Chinese workers immigrated to Hawai'i starting in 1852.

1878 to 1911 / PORTUGUESE

More than 16,000 Portuguese laborers arrived in Hawai'i from 1878 to 1911. Unlike Chinese and Japanese laborers, who were mostly made up of single men, the Portuguese arrived in family units.

workforce. Often the plantations would try to separate people of the same culture, assuming if the workers could not communicate, they could not unionize. Without being able to speak the same language, many of the plantation workers learned to share with each other by using the common language spoken by all: food.

Being on an island in the middle of the ocean, especially in a time when you could not just go online and order ingredients to be delivered to your front door, Hawaiian immigrants had to improvise, adapt, and use what was available. A great example of this is the musubi that has been inspired by a popular Japanese side dish called *omusubi*, which is a ball of rice wrapped in nori and stuffed with a single *ume* (salted plum). By utilizing what was abundant here on the islands, Hawaiian Japanese replaced the ume plum with a salty alternative in the 1980s—Spam. Using the rectangular can as the mold, the famous Hawaiian Spam musubi was created. These "Frankenstein dishes" were created out of necessity to help their creators remember home, and eventually they became the dishes that we modern locals crave when we are away and thinking about home.

1885 to 1924 / JAPANESE

More than 200,000 Japanese laborers immigrated to Hawai'i until the Federal Immigration Act of 1924 shut them out. Today, about 14 percent of Hawai'i's population has Japanese ancestry.

1900 / PUERTO RICANS

Puerto Rican laborers arrived in Hawai'i in 1900. By 1901, more than 5,000 Puerto Ricans had immigrated.

1903 to 1905 / KOREANS

The first significant group of Korean immigrants arrived in 1903 on the RMS Gaelic. Within two years, more than 7,000 Koreans arrived in Hawai'i.

1906 to 1930 / FILIPINOS

The first Filipino laborers arrived in Hawai'i in 1906. Filipinos now surpass the Japanese as the state's largest ethnic group.

Furikake: A mixture of dried seaweed, salt, and sesame, furikake is a common seasoning in Hawaiian food. Nori komi furikake is a furikake blend that is vegetarian and can easily be found online.

Garlic–chili sauce: This is an Indonesian chili paste that goes with everything. Sambal oelek is the most popular type and is available in most grocery stores.

Garlic: Preferably whole cloves for maximum flavor.

Ginger: Fresh gingerroot, peeled and grated, will be frequently used throughout this book.

Mayonnaise: Best Foods or Hellmann's are the preferred brands.

Mochiko flour: This is a sweet rice flour. It does not taste sweet; instead it is made from ground sweet rice. In Hawai'i, it is used in many dishes. Koda Farms brand is the most popular and is easy to find online and may be found at your local market.

Oil: Most of the recipes in this book call for neutral oil, or one that does not have any flavor and works well for both sautéing and frying, such as avocado or canola oil. Sesame oil is also used throughout.

Rice: Calrose short-grain rice is the most popular, but any short-grain variety will do. There are many varieties of rice you could use, ranging from brown rice to bamboo rice; however, when we refer to "rice and mac" in our plate lunches, we are talking about sticky short-grain rice.

Sea salt: Any brand of sea salt will do, and coarse salt melts slower than kosher salt. If you can get Hawaiian sea salt, then choose that.

Soy sauce: In Hawai'i, the most widely used soy sauce (also known as shoyu) is Aloha brand, which has a mellow flavor and is perfect for creating sauces like teriyaki and unagi. Kikkoman is my favorite brand to use on my rice and has a very distinct, deep, roasted flavor; it is used in conjunction with other soy sauces in my recipes to give the extra depth that only Kikkoman can provide. There are gluten-free soy sauces, such as mushroom soy sauce and white soy sauce. Another popular replacement for soy sauce is coconut aminos, which can be found in most health food stores.

Sriracha: The bottle with the rooster is the best and is the original thick chili sauce.

FISH FAQ

When you close your eyes and envision Hawai'i, more than likely you will probably hear the ocean. Hawaiian seafood is known worldwide for its freshness and diversity, from *he'e* (octopus) and *opihi* (limpets) to fresh ahi (tuna), *opakapaka* (Hawaiian snapper), and much, much more. Here are some questions you may have when purchasing seafood.

Q: What should fresh seafood smell like?
A: The first thing is to make sure it doesn't smell too much like seafood. Sounds confusing, but trust me, it really isn't. Fresh seafood should smell fresh and clean with a tiny hint of the ocean. If it smells "fishy," don't buy it.

Q: What should you look for in fresh fish?
A: If you are looking at whole fish, always look at the eyes first: They should be clear and not bloodshot or cloudy. If you are looking at a fillet, you should check for firmness. It should be firm enough to bounce back when pressed slightly.

Q: What is "sushi-grade" poke (fish), and how do you look for it?
A: First you should know that while most sea creatures can be eaten raw, many shouldn't be. Seafood that is great raw includes tuna, salmon, Japanese amberjack (amachi), halibut, clams, and scallops. Fresh is always best, but when eating raw seafood that was frozen, make sure that it was caught properly, bled, and flash-frozen in a short time frame; flash-freezing is used to kill all parasites. Always look for reputable companies. Fish farms in the United States, Japan, Canada, New Zealand, Norway, and Britain all follow strict guidelines for keeping their seafood parasite-free.

A QUICK PRODUCE GUIDE

Being on an island in the middle of the Pacific, the obvious assumption is that we are a seafood-based culture, and while that is true, fresh produce also plays an important role in our cuisine. The first Hawaiians brought a multitude of canoe plants with them to help sustain life and create a thriving culture. Canoe plants include *'olena* (turmeric), kalo (taro), kukui (candle nut), 'uala (sweet potato), and 'ulu (breadfruit). The Hawaiian Islands are

Local Favorites

The following are some of the most popular local foods that I will feature in this book.

Boiled Peanuts: Uncle Charlie was the boiled-peanut maker in our family. We never had to ask who made the boiled peanuts at any party, because we already knew. These treats have a refreshing salty and sweet flavor. Star anise and ginger give the peanuts a robust deliciousness that gets better overnight in the fridge. Most stores here on the islands sell boiled peanuts, and you can even get your boiled peanut fix when you stop at the gas station to fill up your car.

Chicken Katsu: The crispy, light, crunchy coating that comes from the fried panko makes chicken katsu my favorite of all fried chicken. Here in Hawai'i, we have different variations of katsu, such as *tonkatsu* (pork) or ahi katsu (fish); I have even had Spam katsu! This Japanese-inspired dish is best served with a sweet, salty, spicy tomato-based dipping sauce, but you could also smother your chicken katsu in gravy to create an island-style creation known as "chicken cutlet."

Kalua Pig: Kalua pig is the quintessential Hawaiian lū'au dish. The word "kalua" refers to the method of cooking the pork in an imu (underearth oven). This traditional manner of preparing the pork for a feast produces perfect salty, smoked, tender morsels of meat, which trump everything else on a plate lunch, but it can be a time-consuming process.

Loco Moco: If you want to know what we eat for breakfast here in the islands, loco moco would probably be one

Kalua Pig served with stewed cabbage and fresh salad.

Loco Moco is a popular breakfast dish.

of the most popular choices. With two soft hamburger patties over hot white rice topped with an over-easy egg and brown gravy, this meal might put you back to sleep after you eat, but you will probably be dreaming about your breakfast, because it's that good!

Poke: Traditionally served using raw ahi, Hawaiian sea salt, *inamona* (ground kukui nut), and *limu* (seaweed), poke has recently taken on a life of its own. You can now find poke shops in landlocked states such as Colorado, and their versions can include ingredients like tofu and soybeans. Here on the islands, most grocery stores sell a variety of poke, from kimchi *tako* or he'e (octopus) to crab poke and even choices such as cucumber poke and spicy California ahi poke. My version of poke, in this book, closely resembles the shoyu ahi poke that you would find in these stores' poke section.

Sweet and Sour Spareribs: Sweet, sour, sticky, and delicious—the taste of these spareribs is like nothing else. This dish isn't something you find at a lot of Hawaiian plate lunch restaurants because it takes a bit more time and care to prepare. There are different variations of sweet and sour ribs; the Japanese style is brown with pineapple chunks, whereas the Chinese version is red, sweet, and sticky. My version is a combination of the two.

Takuwan: Every bento box (a box with rice, various grilled meats, and fish that is easily transported and packed for a lunch) normally has a piece of *kamaboko* (fishcake) and a slice of takuwan. Takuwan is sweet pickled daikon radish that is dyed light yellow, with chiles sometimes added to make it spicy. Takuwan is the perfect complement to the grilled meats that are served in Hawai'i. Takuwan has a very pungent smell, so make sure to inform the room before cracking open a jar, because people may look at you funny if they don't know that it's a delicious condiment.

Takuwan, a sweet pickled daikon (radish).

volcanic and were created from a hot spot in the Pacific. The Big Island (Hawai'i) is made up of five volcanos; two are still active, and as I write this, Kilauea is erupting. To save you from a science lesson and botany jargon, I will just say that basically the volcanic ground is porous and full of minerals, so the plants of Hawai'i thrive and are full of nutrients.

When trying to pick out excellent produce in the store, aside from the obvious such as no blemishes or bruising, you should check the scent. I know this sounds crazy, and you might not want to be that person sniffing a pineapple in the supermarket, but when tropical fruit is ripe, it smells wonderful and you can tell that it is ready to eat. A rule of thumb I use when looking for produce is to follow the mantra "size matters," and no, it is not in the way you think. Usually, the smaller the vegetable, the more flavor and nutrition it packs, so instead of looking for the biggest pineapple in the bunch, look for the most colorful (golden in the pineapple's case), firm, and yes, the best-smelling one.

In this book I will be using some tropical fruits such as pineapple and mango, but for the most part, the produce used in these recipes should be available everywhere. If something a little more exotic is required (for example, taro or purple sweet potato), I will be sure to give you some alternatives.

TOOLS AND EQUIPMENT

In this book, I deliberately try to keep the necessary tools to a minimum. There are some tools that you will be using more than others. For the most part, you probably already have the tools required to make these dishes, but keeping them available, sharp, and clean will make all the difference in the world.

Essentials

Baking sheet. Honestly, whatever is affordable will do. The prices will vary with thickness and material, but if you are careful, you should be able to make do with any type of baking sheet.

Knives. A chef's knife, a bread knife, and a paring knife are the most important, and you can basically get away with just those three.

Pots. Large heavy-bottomed pots are a must, and you need at least one good nonstick pan that is six inches or larger in diameter.

Rice cooker. If you love rice and/or plan to eat like a Hawaiian, a rice cooker is essential. The most important reason for a rice cooker is not for just cooking the rice (it does a dandy job of it though!); it also does amazing job of keeping rice warm for your midday or midnight snack.

Time-Savers

Blender or food processor. These can help you create smooth sauces, chop onions, and dice aromatics efficiently.

Mortar and pestle. A few of the recipes call for a mortar and pestle, but if you don't have one, a quick pulse in the food processor (or often even a smash from the bottom of a heavy pan, in the case of peppercorns) will work just as well.

READY FOR ONO GRINDS?

Throughout this book, you'll find the following labels to help you navigate the recipes:

5-INGREDIENT: These recipes call for five ingredients, not including salt, pepper, or oil/ cooking spray/butter.

ONE-POT: You can create these recipes using just one pot/pan from start to finish.

QUICK: These recipes take 30 minutes or fewer to prep and cook.

This book includes a chapter on homemade staples. Whenever a recipe calls for a homemade item, it will also include a shortcut tip to replace it with a premade version of that item.

You'll also find tips for flexibility. These will suggest lighter/healthier meals, different variations, or serving/pairing suggestions.

Ohana Spirit: Four Menus to Try

THE BACKYARD POTLUCK

Pā'ina, parties or potlucks, were practically a weekly thing for my family when I was younger. I do not think that I can stress it enough in this book that Hawaiian food is meant to bring people together! The pā'ina at my grandma's house were just an excuse for everyone to get together and visit with ohana while eating ono (tasty) food that was happily prepared by my aunties and uncles. Typical dishes brought to a potluck might include:

» Hawaiian Fruit Punch (page 33)

» Boiled Peanuts (page 18)

» Namasu (page 25)

» Musubi (page 27)

» Chicken Katsu (page 48)

» Spicy Crab and Rice Party Pan (page 68)

» Banana Cream Parfait (page 93)

BEACH DAY

Beach days are something that everyone born or living in Hawai'i knows well. The beaches here are our Museum of Natural History or Museum of Modern Art. My family used to go down to Hapuna Beach almost weekly when I was a kid. One thing that was always the same were the snacks. My mom would make Spam musubi and cut up tropical fruits while my dad loaded the car. Typical dishes brought to a beach day might include:

» Musubi (page 27)

» Teriyaki Chicken (page 47)

» Hawaiian Teriyaki Barbecue Beef (page 40)

» Hibachi Beach Pork (page 51)

» Hawaiian Fruit Punch (page 33)

DATE NIGHT

Date nights for me usually include some sort of interactive cooking activity that you can do together. I am lucky because my beautiful wife is also a chef, and aside from her amazing personality and radiant beauty, it is true when they say "the way to a man's heart is through his stomach," because I was in love with my wife from the moment she cooked me that first meal! Typical dishes for date night:

» Cone Sushi (page 22)

» Spicy Ahi Poke Bowls (page 19)

» "Whatever You Like" Fried Rice (page 29)

» Miso Salmon (page 62)

» Namasu (page 25)

» Polynesian Limeade (page 32)

HOLIDAY PARTY

I am focusing a little more on Christmas and New Year's with this menu. Christmas was always spent at home with my parents celebrating my Southern Italian heritage from my mom's side with the Feast of the Seven Fishes on Christmas Eve, although we still had our delicious local-style goodies on Christmas Day. New Year's was a big deal in our family, and everyone would go either to my grandma's or Uncle Scotty's house. There would be a table (or multiple tables) laden with food; everyone contributed. My uncles and aunties would drink beer and play the ukulele and guitar while singing Hawaiian songs. These are truly some of my fondest food memories, and I continue to try and create similar moments with my cousins and friends. Typical dishes brought to a holiday party:

» Prune Mui (page 91)

» Hurricane Popcorn (page 86)

» Furikake Party Mix (page 94)

» Boiled Peanuts (page 18)

» Takuwan (page 20)

» Portuguese Pickled Onions (page 24)

» Mom's Chinese Oxtail Soup (Local Style) (page 54)

» Ice Cake (page 89)

All About Mixed Plates

When you go to a Hawaiian plate lunch restaurant and are looking up at the menu, nine times out of ten you are going to think "How do I decide what to get?" Well, you aren't the only person to think this, and we all have a section of our menu to help remedy that issue and it's called "mixed plates." A mixed plate is usually made up of two different proteins (sometimes three) with your rice and potato mac salad all on one plate. Growing up my all-time favorite mixed plate was teriyaki beef and tempura mahi-mahi. I would dip my beef in the tartar sauce, and it is still one of my guilty pleasures to this day. My wife always goes for the chicken katsu and kalua pig. My little brother does the kalbi (short ribs) and garlic shrimp, and my dad loves his Korean pork and chicken katsu. Mixed plate is the perfect way to get a little taste of everything you want. Try it out for yourself at home! Using the following suggestions from the book, choose a couple recipes and try making your next meal a truly traditional "mixed plate."

Choose your mains:
» Chicken Katsu (page 48)
» Kalua Pig and Cabbage (page 45)
» Hawaiian Teriyaki Barbecue Beef (page 40)
» Lemon Chicken (page 42)
» Orange Chicken (page 52)
» Shoyu Chicken (page 38)
» Hamburger Steak (page 56)
» Masayo's "Paniolo" Beef Stew (page 39)
» Nori-Crusted Mahi-Mahi with Wasabi Aioli (page 63)
» Miso Salmon (page 62)

Add a side:
» Potato Mac Salad (page 21)
» Namasu (page 25)
» Portuguese Pickled Onions (page 24)
» Takuwan (page 20)
» Lomi Salmon (page 28)
» "Whatever You Like" Fried Rice (page 29)

Musubi PAGE 27,
Hawaiian Fruit
Punch PAGE 33

CHAPTER TWO

Small Bites and Drinks

BOILED PEANUTS

5-INGREDIENT ONE-POT

Prep time: 5 minutes, plus overnight to soak / **Cook time:** 1 hour, plus 1 hour to cool
Serves 4 to 6

These are one of my dad's favorite snacks and a staple at every pā'ina (party). The best part is eating them after they are chilled and getting the burst of flavor from all the liquid trapped in the shells. These flavors bring me back to the memory of my dad playing the ukulele and everyone singing along while I happily cracked open my peanut shells.

2 pounds raw shell-on peanuts

4 quarts water

⅓ cup salt

3 whole star anise

3 whole cloves

1 (3-inch) piece fresh ginger, cut into ½-inch-thick rounds

1. In a colander, rinse the peanuts thoroughly.

2. In a pot or bowl, combine the clean peanuts, water, salt, anise, and cloves. Place a bowl or plate on top to make sure the peanuts are fully submerged. Soak the peanuts at room temperature overnight, or up to 24 hours.

3. In a large pot, combine the soaked peanuts, the soaking water and spices, and the ginger. Bring to a boil over high, then reduce to medium-low heat. Simmer for 1 hour, checking for doneness by taking a peanut out of its shell and eating it. It should be soft with a little bite to it.

4. Remove the pot from the heat and allow to cool for at least 1 hour. Serve warm, at room temperature, or chilled, with an empty bowl for the shells. Store in an airtight container or bag for up to 5 days in the refrigerator.

Ingredient Smarts: Look for shell-on peanuts at Asian markets or online stores.

SPICY AHI POKE BOWLS

QUICK

Prep time: 10 minutes / **Serves 4**

Poke has always been popular in Hawai'i. Here you can go to most grocery stores and find a nice selection of poke to choose from. No matter what type of party I serve this poke at, whether it's at a million-dollar beachfront home or my grandma's backyard for New Year's, it is always a hit. Feel free to add 1 teaspoon of sambal oelek to the poke if you like spice, or sprinkle with furikake for even more flavor.

FOR THE POKE

2 pounds fresh ahi tuna, cut into 1-inch cubes*

2 teaspoons kosher salt

3 tablespoons low-sodium soy sauce

1 tablespoon sugar

1 teaspoon sesame oil

1 garlic clove, minced

2 teaspoons minced fresh ginger

2 scallions, green parts only, cut diagonally

Cooked white rice, for serving

½ avocado, cubed

FOR THE AIOLI

½ cup mayonnaise

2 tablespoons sriracha

Dash mirin

1. **TO MAKE THE POKE:** In a large bowl, add the ahi and salt and mix to combine. Allow to sit for at least 5 minutes for the salt to absorb.

2. In a separate bowl, whisk together the soy sauce, sugar, sesame oil, garlic, ginger, and scallions. Pour the sauce over the tuna and mix well.

3. **TO MAKE THE AIOLI:** In a small bowl, mix the mayonnaise, sriracha, and mirin.

4. Serve the poke on a bed of hot rice, topped with avocado and a drizzle of the spicy aioli.

*Try This: You can use medium-firm tofu or any other sashimi-grade seafood instead of tuna.

TAKUWAN

5-INGREDIENT   ONE-POT

Prep time: 20 minutes, plus 2 days to pickle / **Cook time:** 5 minutes / **Makes 1 quart**

Takuwan (pickled daikon radishes) is served in just about every bento here on the islands. Growing up, I would eat it right out of the jar; the problem is that when you open it, the entire house knows because of its distinctive smell. Don't let the smell fool you, though—this side dish is delicious and the perfect accompaniment to most grilled meats.

1 cup water

1 cup sugar

¼ cup rice vinegar

1 tablespoon salt

3 drops yellow food coloring (optional)

4 daikon radishes (about 2 pounds), cut into ¼-inch rounds

Chili pepper flakes (optional)

1. In a large pot, combine the water, sugar, vinegar, and salt. Heat over medium heat until the sugar is just dissolved (no need to boil). Turn off the heat and let the liquid cool.

2. Add the food coloring (if using) and stir to combine.

3. Place the daikon and chili pepper flakes (if using) in a jar and pour the cooled pickling liquid over top. Seal the jar and transfer to the refrigerator.

4. The daikon will be ready in 2 days but will taste best if enjoyed after 1 week. Store in the refrigerator for up to 3 weeks.

Ingredient Smarts: If you wanted to use these for sandwiches instead of eating as a side, feel free to cut the daikon into ½-by-3-inch matchsticks instead of rounds.

POTATO MAC SALAD

QUICK

Prep time: 15 minutes, plus cooling time / **Cook time:** 15 minutes / **Serves 4**

The perfect accompaniment to just about any dish in this book, Potato Mac Salad is like kimchi or marinara sauce: Every family has their version, and their version is better than everyone else's. This salad must be made with Best Foods brand mayonnaise (or Hellmann's on the East Coast). The eggs are grated to add extra richness, and the onions and celery are blended in a food processor to create more flavor throughout.

3 russet potatoes

8 ounces dry elbow macaroni pasta

1 celery stalk, trimmed

½ yellow onion, roughly chopped

2 cups mayonnaise, divided

4 large hard-boiled eggs

⅓ cup grated carrot

1 teaspoon salt

½ teaspoon freshly ground black pepper

1. In a large pot, add the potatoes with enough water to cover. Bring the potatoes to a boil and cook until fork tender, about 15 minutes. Drain, cool, peel, and cut the potatoes into 1-inch cubes.

2. Meanwhile, boil the macaroni according to package instructions. Drain and allow to cool and dry.

3. In a food processor, add the celery and onion. Process until well minced. Squeeze out any excess liquid and set aside.

4. Put the potatoes in a large bowl, add 1 cup of mayonnaise and mix, allowing the potato to break up just a little. Grate the eggs over the potato and mayonnaise. Add the cooked macaroni. Fold in the remaining 1 cup of mayonnaise, the celery and onion mixture, and the carrot, salt, and pepper until the macaroni is coated and everything is incorporated evenly. Taste and add more salt and pepper if needed. Serve chilled.

CONE SUSHI

Prep time: 30 minutes, plus cooling time / **Cook time:** 35 minutes / **Serves 6**

This is Aunty Clara and Aunty Vivian's special recipe. The sweet and salty sushi rice encased in fluffy abura-age, or Japanese fried bean curd, creates a treat that you will not soon forget. Top this with the poke from the Spicy Ahi Poke Bowls (page 19), and you get the extremely popular "poke bomb." I still don't know if it gets its name from its little grenade-like shape or the fact that it explodes with flavor.

FOR THE SUSHI RICE

4 cups cooked white short-grain rice

½ cup rice vinegar

½ cup sugar

1 tablespoon salt

FOR THE ABURA-AGE

9 abura-age, cut in half diagonally

8 cups water

2 tablespoons dashi granules

6 dried shrimp (optional)

1 cup sugar

1 teaspoon salt

3 teaspoons mirin

8 teaspoons soy sauce

¼ cup finely shredded carrot (about ½ carrot)

1. **TO MAKE THE SUSHI RICE:** In a large bowl, place the freshly cooked hot white rice.

2. In a small saucepan, combine the vinegar, sugar, and salt. Heat over low heat until the sugar is just dissolved. Turn off the heat and allow the liquid to come to room temperature.

3. Gently fan the rice while slowly adding the vinegar mixture. Add the sauce a little a time, fold the rice, and fan. Repeat until you use all the liquid. Cover the sushi rice with a lightly damp towel and set aside for at least 1 hour to cool.

4. **TO MAKE THE ABURA-AGE:** In a medium pot, cover the abura-age with water and simmer for about 3 minutes over medium heat to render the fat. Drain the abura-age and transfer to a bowl. Set aside.

5. In the same pot, combine the 8 cups of water, dashi, dried shrimp (if using), sugar, salt, mirin, and soy sauce. Bring to a simmer over medium-high heat and add the drained abura-age. Cook for 30 minutes and strain, reserving the liquid. Gently squeeze out any extra liquid from the abura-age. Set aside to cool.

6. Pour the reserved liquid into a small pot, and over high heat, boil the carrot for about 5 minutes, until soft, and drain. Fold the carrot into the sushi rice.

7. Once cooled, on a clean work surface, open the cut side of the abura-age to create a pouch, like a pita. Stuff the rice-carrot mixture into each abura-age pocket. Repeat with the rest of the rice and abura-age and serve.

PORTUGUESE PICKLED ONIONS

Prep time: 15 minutes, plus 24 hours to pickle / **Cook time:** 5 minutes / **Makes 1 quart**

These sweet, salty, and sour pickled onions aren't your typical pickles, but I promise, you can't knock it till you try it. The pickling process brings out the natural sugar from the onion and creates a light but complex flavor. This pickle goes especially well with Masayo's "Paniolo" Beef Stew (page 39).

2 or 3 onions, cut into
½-inch cubes

½ carrot, cut into
¼-inch-thick sticks

1 bell pepper, cut into
½-inch strips

1 garlic clove, crushed
(optional)

2 teaspoons chili pepper
flakes (optional)

1½ cups water

1½ cups distilled
white vinegar

½ cup sugar

1 tablespoon salt

1. In a glass jar, combine the onions, carrot, bell pepper, garlic (if using), and chili flakes (if using).

2. In a saucepan, combine the water, vinegar, sugar, and salt and bring to a boil over medium-high heat. Once the brine is boiling, turn off the heat and pour the hot brine over the vegetables in the jar. Set aside to cool.

3. Seal and refrigerate for at least 24 hours before enjoying. Keep refrigerated for up to 3 weeks.

NAMASU

Prep time: 15 minutes, plus 24 hours to pickle / **Cook time:** 5 minutes / **Makes 1 quart**

Namasu is not your typical pickle; it is a little more delicate. Often served in small bowls as an accompaniment to Japanese meals, these pickles were a staple in our house. My mom loves Namasu, and we always had a mason jar in the fridge just in case guests came over.

---

1 English cucumber or 2 Japanese cucumbers, sliced into ¼-inch rounds

1 carrot, julienned into ⅛-by-3-inch pieces

½ cup rice vinegar

⅓ cup water

⅓ cup sugar

1 teaspoon salt

1 (¼-inch) piece fresh ginger (optional)

½ teaspoon sesame seeds

1. Put the cucumber and carrot in a glass jar.

2. In a saucepan, combine the vinegar, water, sugar, salt, and ginger (if using). Heat over medium-high until the sugar and salt are just dissolved. Pour the brine over the cucumber and carrot and add the sesame seeds. Set aside to cool.

3. Seal and refrigerate for at least 24 hours before enjoying. Keep refrigerated for up to 2 weeks.

GARLIC AND SESAME EDAMAME

QUICK

Prep time: 5 minutes / **Cook time:** 5 minutes / **Serves 4**

These soybeans are delicious and pair perfectly with a cold beer. Garlicky, spicy, and sweet, these snacks are great for pau hana *(happy hour) but maybe not a first date (the garlic can be rough for a first kiss). You can adjust this recipe based on your preference and make it as spicy or sweet as you like.*

2 pounds edamame, in shell

2 garlic cloves, minced

1 tablespoon minced fresh ginger

2 teaspoons sesame oil

1 tablespoon soy sauce

2 teaspoons sugar

1 teaspoon sambal oelek

1. In a large pot, boil the edamame in salted water for 5 minutes, or according to package instructions. Drain and set aside to cool.

2. In a large bowl, combine the garlic, ginger, sesame oil, soy sauce, sugar, and sambal oelek and mix well. Stir in the edamame. Toss to coat well and serve.

MUSUBI

QUICK

Prep time: 15 minutes / **Cook time:** 5 minutes / **Serves 4**

Found at every Hawaiian grocery store and gas station, Musubi is like the hot dog of Hawai'i. It's the perfect portable meal for the beach, in the car, or at work. When I was growing up, every weekend that my family wasn't going to Hilo to visit my grandma, we would go to the beach with our Tupperware full of Musubi. You can easily find a musubi mold online.

1 cup Teriyaki Sauce (page 105)*

1 tablespoon Cornstarch Slurry (page 102)

1 to 2 teaspoons neutral oil

1 (12-ounce) can Spam, cut horizontally into 8 slices

8 sheets nori wrapping paper

5 to 6 cups cooked white medium- or short-grain rice

Ingredient Smarts: To get a little more seasoning on your Musubi, use my mother's trick: Get a bowl of salted water and rub the water lightly on your (clean) hands while making the musubi—particularly when adding the rice.

1. In a small saucepan, bring the teriyaki sauce to a simmer over medium heat. Slowly stir in the cornstarch slurry, whisking constantly, until the sauce thickens. Remove from the heat and set aside.

2. In a nonstick pan or skillet, heat the oil over medium-high heat and sear the Spam on both sides for about 3 minutes, until nice and crispy. Transfer to a plate and set aside.

3. On a clean work surface, place the nori, rough side facing up. Place a musubi mold centered on the piece of nori.

4. Put some rice into the mold and press down with the top of a musubi maker (the rice should be a little less than halfway up the musubi mold). Place the Spam on the rice and rub with about 1 teaspoon of the teriyaki glaze. Add more rice on top and press down, making sure the rice does not spill out of the mold.

5. With the top is pressed down, firmly lift the mold up and gently remove the top. Wrap the nori up around the molded rice, bringing both ends to the middle. Use a tiny bit of water on your finger to moisten the end of the nori to stick it to the other side. Repeat with the rest of the Spam, rice, and sauce.

*****Shortcut:** Use store-bought teriyaki sauce to save time.

LOMI SALMON

5-INGREDIENT

Prep time: 2 hours, plus overnight to refrigerate / **Serves 4 to 6**

Lomi Salmon is sure to be on the menu at every tourist lū'au you attend, but locals love it, too. My absolute favorite way to eat it is in a bowl mixed with some kalua pig, cabbage, and poi (taro root paste). Lomi lomi means "to massage" in Hawaiian, and that is a key part of this dish. The salted salmon acts as the seasoning for this dish, and the mixing process seasons the onion and tomatoes to create the perfect balance of acid, spice, and salt.

8 ounces salmon fillet

¼ cup kosher salt

5 Roma tomatoes, seeded and diced

1 large sweet onion, diced

5 scallions, green parts only, cut diagonally

½ teaspoon Chili Pepper Water (page 98)*

1. Place the salmon fillet in a large bowl and rub it with the salt. Cover and refrigerate overnight.

2. The next day, rinse the fish and soak it in an ice bath for 1 hour. Dice the salmon into ¼-inch cubes.

3. In a large bowl, combine the salmon cubes, tomatoes, onion, scallions, and chili pepper water and mix. Cover and refrigerate for 1 hour before serving.

*Shortcut: If you can't find chili pepper water or don't feel like making your own, feel free to omit it from this recipe. If you still want to add something spicy, two dashes of Tabasco would work.

"WHATEVER YOU LIKE" FRIED RICE

ONE-POT

Prep time: 20 minutes / **Cook time:** 30 minutes / **Serves 4 to 6**

The name says it all. You can literally put whatever you like in this fried rice. Here I'm using vegetables, but you could add Spam, kalua pork, chicken, teriyaki beef, bacon, or char siu—the possibilities are endless. With this easy recipe, you will be on your way to making your version of fried rice with whatever you have leftover in the refrigerator.

1 tablespoon neutral oil

1 cup diced carrots

½ yellow onion, minced

1 red bell pepper, diced

½ cup chopped scallions, both white and green parts

3 garlic cloves, finely chopped

1 tablespoon sesame oil

3 cups cooked rice, chilled overnight

2 tablespoons soy sauce

1 tablespoon oyster sauce

1 teaspoon Worcestershire sauce

1 tablespoon hoisin sauce (optional)

1 large egg, beaten

Salt

Freshly ground black pepper

1. In a wok or large nonstick sauté pan, heat the oil over medium heat and cook the carrots for about 5 minutes, until they are tender. Add the onion and cook for another 5 minutes, until it is translucent. Add the bell pepper and scallions and cook for another 3 minutes, until soft.

2. Add the garlic and sesame oil and mix to combine. Add the rice, breaking it up with a wooden spoon or spatula. Stir in the soy sauce, oyster sauce, Worcestershire sauce, and hoisin sauce (if using). Cook over medium heat for 3 to 5 more minutes, allowing the rice to absorb most of the liquid.

3. Once all the liquid is absorbed and the rice is hot and a nice even color, create a well in the center of the rice and add the beaten egg, allowing it to cook for 2 minutes. Mix the egg into the rice so that the hot rice scrambles the egg.

4. Once the egg is cooked, season with salt and pepper to taste. Serve immediately.

Ingredient Smarts: If you like a little more spice, feel free to add 1 tablespoon of sambal oelek or a few dashes of your favorite hot sauce. There is no way to make this recipe wrong because *your* way is the right way.

MAI TAI

Prep time: 2 minutes / **Serves 1**

The Mai Tai cocktail is famous for not only its tiki bar vibe but also the infamous debate on who invented it: Trader Vic or Don the Beachcomber? Although we may never agree on who made the original, we can all agree that a Mai Tai is perfect for a hot summer day at the beach!

2 ounces white rum

¾ ounce orange curaçao

¾ ounce freshly
   squeezed lime juice

½ ounce orgeat syrup

Ice

½ ounce dark rum

1. In a cocktail shaker, combine the white rum, curaçao, lime juice, and orgeat syrup. Add ice and shake well.

2. Strain and pour over a double rocks glass filled with ice.

3. Slowly pour the dark rum on top to create a "float" and serve.

Ingredient Smarts: To help with the float, hold a spoon upside-down right over your drink. Slowly pour the dark rum over the back of the spoon; this will disperse the rum and create a perfect float.

LAVA FLOW

Prep time: 10 minutes / **Serves 4 to 6**

As a kid growing up in Hawai'i, whenever we went on our family "staycations" at the hotels along the golden coast of the Big Island, my favorite thing was a virgin Lava Flow. Call it cliché but the strawberry puree running down the insides of the glass really does give it a lava-like feel (okay, maybe more like a lava lamp than a volcano). Enjoy this resort classic any time of the year with this tasty recipe.

4 ounces strawberries

4 ounces coconut rum

6 ounces white rum

6 ounces cream of coconut

6 ounces pineapple juice

½ cup frozen pineapple chunks

4 cups ice

1. In a blender, blend the strawberries and coconut rum until smooth. Pour the mixture into cups, turning the cups as you pour and letting the strawberry puree run down the inside of the glass; this will give the "lava" effect.

2. In a clean blender, combine the white rum, cream of coconut, pineapple juice, frozen pineapple (make sure it is fully frozen), and ice and blend until smooth.

3. Pour over the strawberry puree and enjoy.

Ingredient Smarts: Top this with some fresh pineapple, a maraschino cherry, and a paper parasol to create the perfect Hawaiian party drink.

POLYNESIAN LIMEADE

5-INGREDIENT   ONE-POT   QUICK

Prep time: 5 minutes / **Cook time:** 5 minutes / **Serves 6**

My mom used to serve this at her Italian restaurant in Waimea. It was so popular that we would have to make a five-gallon batch almost every day! The coconut extract brings a real "nose" to this drink so you are smelling coconut while sipping it, stimulating multiple senses at once. Serve this in a big pitcher with slices of fresh lime.

¼ cup sugar

48 ounces plus ¼ cup water, divided

1 (12-ounce) can Minute Maid limeade concentrate

½ teaspoon coconut extract

1. In a saucepan over medium-high heat, dissolve the sugar in ¼ cup of water and bring to a quick boil to create a simple syrup. As soon as it boils, remove from the heat and let cool.

2. In a pitcher, mix the limeade concentrate, the remaining 48 ounces of water, coconut extract, and simple syrup. Mix and enjoy.

Ingredient Smarts: You can use any type of limeade; however, depending on the brand, you will have to adjust the amount of water and sugar. To make a super easy version of this recipe, buy an already-prepared ½ gallon of limeade and just add the coconut extract.

HAWAIIAN FRUIT PUNCH

5-INGREDIENT **ONE-POT** **QUICK**

Prep time: 5 minutes / **Serves 6**

Now this might not be as sweet as the classic Hawaiian Punch with the little surfing guy on the front. Don't get me wrong—I love that fruit punch—but this is a bit more in line with my style. When I make this for parties, I use the rest of the guava juice to make ice cubes so that when they melt, the punch only gets better!

½ cup sugar*
½ cup water
2 cups guava nectar
2 cups no-pulp orange juice
1½ cups pineapple juice
Juice of 1 lemon

1. In a saucepan over medium-high heat, dissolve the sugar in the water and bring to a quick boil to create a simple syrup. As soon as it boils, remove from the heat and let cool.

2. In a large pitcher, mix the guava nectar, orange juice, pineapple juice, lemon juice, and simple syrup and enjoy.

*Try This: Add more sugar or lemon juice to taste. Also, if you want your punch a little thicker, you can add strawberry puree to the orange juice and mix well.

Hawaiian Teriyaki Barbecue
Beef PAGE 40

CHAPTER THREE

Chicken, Pork, and Beef

SWEET AND SOUR SPARERIBS

ONE-POT

Prep time: 15 minutes / **Cook time:** 2 hours 30 minutes / **Serves 4**

This sweet, sour, and sticky dish is finger-licking deliciousness. This recipe resembles the Chinese preparation, with the addition of a little fresh pineapple inspired by the Japanese version to help cut through all the richness. Spareribs are from the lower portion of the pig behind the shoulder, not to be confused with beef short ribs. This dish is best served with acidic sides like Portuguese Pickled Onions (page 24) or Namasu (page 25) to complement the sweetness of the ribs.

4 pounds spareribs, cut into 2- or 3-inch cubes and rinsed

2 (1-inch) pieces fresh ginger

4 cups water

2½ cups sugar

1½ cups vinegar*

¾ cup ketchup

2 tablespoons soy sauce*

½ cup canned pineapple chunks, plus more for garnish

Cooking Tip: When cooking this dish down for the last 30 minutes in step 2, if you notice that the sauce is too thick for you, feel free to add a little water anytime during the cooking process.

1. Put the spareribs in large pot, cover with water, and simmer over medium to medium-low heat for 1 hour. Drain in a colander and rinse very well.

2. Return the cooked, rinsed spareribs to the pot and add the ginger, water, sugar, vinegar, ketchup, soy sauce, and pineapple. Bring to a simmer and cook, covered, for 30 minutes. Uncover and cook for another 30 minutes, or until the spareribs are soft.

3. Remove the pot from the heat and allow the ribs to sit for about 20 minutes to let the fat rise to the top. Using a ladle, skim off the excess fat and discard. (You can also put the pot in the refrigerator and chill for about 30 minutes to allow the fat to solidify on top, making it easier to remove and discard.) Return the pot to the stove and bring it back up to temperature over medium-high heat until hot.

4. Garnish with some fresh pineapple before serving.

*Try This: Distilled white vinegar, rice vinegar, or apple cider vinegar work equally well here. Instead of soy sauce, try 1½ tablespoons of dark soy sauce instead. Lee Kum Kee brand is easily found online if you can't find it at your local market.

PORK ADOBO

ONE-POT

Prep time: 10 minutes / **Cook time:** 1 hour 20 minutes / **Serves 4**

Ask any Filipino, "Who makes the best adobo?" and they will say, "My mom, of course." Now, I am not here to "throw down" with anyone's nana, but I will say my adobo can compete. My little secret is Dijon mustard, which adds a delicious flavor to the dish, and because there is already vinegar in the adobo, it blends perfectly. Serve this recipe over a bowl of hot rice with some Takuwan (page 20) and some Potato Mac Salad (page 21).

2 tablespoons neutral oil

2½ pounds pork butt, cut into 1½-inch cubes

1 tablespoon Dijon mustard

4 garlic cloves, minced

2 cups water

1 cup vinegar*

½ cup soy sauce

1 teaspoon whole peppercorns

3 bay leaves

1 tablespoon brown sugar

1 scallion, green parts only, cut diagonally, for garnish

1. In a large pot, heat the oil over medium heat until shimmering. Add the pork and cook for about 5 minutes, until lightly browned on all sides.

2. Add the Dijon mustard and garlic and quickly stir together.

3. Add the water, vinegar, soy sauce, peppercorns, and bay leaves to the pot. Bring to a simmer and cook, covered, for 45 minutes. Uncover and continue to cook at a gentle simmer for another 30 minutes, until the gravy starts to reduce and thicken. Don't rush this; avoid cooking it over high heat. Remember: Low and slow wins the race when it comes to adobo.

4. After 25 minutes of simmering, add the brown sugar and mix in well. Simmer until the sugar is melted into the sauce, about 5 more minutes. Remove and discard the bay leaves, garnish with the scallions, and serve.

*Try This: Use either rice vinegar, apple cider vinegar, or distilled white vinegar.

Ingredient Smarts: If you prefer a creamier sauce, substitute 1 cup of coconut milk for 1 cup of the water.

SHOYU CHICKEN

Prep time: 5 minutes / **Cook time:** 50 minutes / **Serves 4**

Juicy chicken thighs, lightly simmered in a sweet and salty sauce, until the meat is soft and pulls apart easily . . . Shoyu Chicken is the best! It's the best not just because it tastes like a Hawaiian backyard potluck but also because it is so easy to make. When I was little, one of my favorite snacks after school was putting a scoop of rice in a Chinese saimin bowl and heading over to the warming table to pour some shoyu chicken gravy all over it.

6 to 8 skin-on, bone-in chicken thighs

6 cups Teriyaki Sauce (page 105)*

3 tablespoons Cornstarch Slurry (page 102)

4 cups cooked white rice

2 scallions, green parts only, cut diagonally, for garnish

2 teaspoons sesame seeds, for garnish

1. In a large pot, add the chicken and cover with the teriyaki sauce, making sure the chicken is fully covered by the liquid.

2. Cover and let simmer over medium heat for about 45 minutes, or until the chicken is fully cooked and soft enough to pull apart. Cooking times can vary, so the best way is to check the chicken for tenderness. Avoid cooking at a rolling boil, or your chicken will be dry and the skin will fall off.

3. Remove the chicken from the pot and set aside in a bowl or plate, then bring the sauce to a simmer. Add the cornstarch slurry to the pot slowly, a little at a time, while whisking. Let thicken to the consistency of gravy or until it can coat the back of a spoon.

4. To serve, place the chicken over the hot rice and pour over the thickened glaze. Garnish with scallions and sesame seeds.

*Shortcut: Use a store-bought teriyaki sauce to save time.

MASAYO'S "PANIOLO" BEEF STEW

ONE-POT

Prep time: 30 minutes / **Cook time:** 2 hours / **Serves 4**

This recipe is especially important to me. Growing up at Dad's plate lunch restaurant, the main chef who cooked everything was named Masayo. Her nickname was the "kitchen magician," and she spent most of her life cooking in a restaurant. She was a very important part of our family and inspired me to become a chef. This beef stew recipe is not fancy; it doesn't have any hand-crushed San Marzano tomatoes or torn cilantro, nor does it include beef bouillon. Instead we use the meat, water, and ketchup to create her delicious stew. This recipe is simple and perfect, just like the woman who taught me how to cook it. "Mama" Masayo is no longer with us, but her recipes and influence on my culinary career will continue to flourish and be shared with anyone who is willing to listen and learn. Paniolo are the Hawaiian cowboys that were trained by Spanish colonists; their thriving culture is still strong in my hometown of Waimea.

2 pounds chuck roast, cut into 2-inch cubes

12 cups water, divided

2 teaspoons salt

1 large onion, cut in half, and then each half cut into 6 pieces

3 celery stalks, cut into 2-inch pieces

2 garlic cloves, smashed

2 teaspoons tomato paste

⅓ cup ketchup

1 teaspoon freshly ground black pepper

2 jumbo carrots, peeled and cut into 2-inch chunks (roll cut)

2 large russet potatoes, peeled and cut into 1-inch cubes

1. In a large pot, rinse the meat well and drain.

2. Return the rinsed meat to the pot and add 11 cups of water and the salt. Bring to a boil over medium heat and cook for 45 minutes. While simmering, skim off the fat and bubbles from the top.

3. Add the onion, celery, and garlic and simmer for another 25 minutes.

4. Add the remaining 1 cup of water, the tomato paste, ketchup, and pepper and mix well.

5. Add the carrots and cook for another 20 to 40 minutes, or until the carrots start to get soft and fork-tender.

6. Finally, add the potatoes and cook until the potatoes are soft and easily pierced through with a knife, about 10 minutes.

Ingredient Smarts: If you want more stew "gravy," add 3 more cups of water in the beginning, then add Cornstarch Slurry (page 102) to thicken it to your liking.

HAWAIIAN TERIYAKI BARBECUE BEEF

Prep time: 5 minutes, plus 24 hours to marinate / **Cook time:** 15 minutes / **Serves 4**

On our menu we have a teriyaki beef burger, and it is described as "Chef Ippy's favorite sandwich." That isn't just to sell more burgers (although it helps). This thinly sliced marinated beef is extremely popular in Hawai'i. You can serve the teriyaki on a bun with lettuce, tomato, mayo, and onion as a burger. It's also delicious as a plate lunch with hot white rice and Potato Mac Salad (page 21).

2 pounds thinly sliced
beef chuck*

4 cups Teriyaki Sauce
(page 105), divided*

1 tablespoon neutral oil

3 tablespoons Cornstarch
Slurry (page 102)

1. Place the beef in a nonreactive bowl or Tupperware, making sure that the beef is not bloody and that it is somewhat dry, as too much blood will dilute the marinade and water it down. Separate each piece so the marinade can permeate.

2. Add 2 cups of teriyaki sauce so the meat is fully covered. Cover, refrigerate, and let soak for at least 24 hours.

3. In a large pan, heat the oil over medium-high heat, add a slice of beef, and cook for about 3 minutes on each side. Because of the sugar in the marinade, it will caramelize a bit. Don't worry—the caramelization will add more flavor. Continue with the rest of the pieces.

4. In a small saucepan, bring the remaining 2 cups of teriyaki sauce to a simmer over medium heat. Slowly add the cornstarch slurry, a little at a time, whisking continuously. Allow it to thicken to the consistency of gravy, or until it can coat the back of a spoon, about 5 minutes.

5. Glaze the cooked meat with the thickened sauce and serve.

*Try This: Feel free to replace the thinly sliced beef with any of your favorite steaks like rib eye, New York, flank, or skirt steak.

*Shortcut: Use a store-bought teriyaki sauce to save time.

MOCHIKO CHICKEN

Prep time: 15 minutes, plus 3 hours to marinate / **Cook time:** 20 minutes / **Serves 4**

Mochiko Chicken gets its name from the mochi flour (sweet rice flour) that is used to make it. Mochiko has a strong standing history when looking at the unique foods of Hawai'i. The sweet, crispy chicken has many different adaptations, though in this recipe I dredge the chicken in flour and cornstarch to give it a crispy crunch. However, some people just put the chicken directly into the fryer straight out of the marinade to create a stickier texture.

FOR THE CHICKEN

2 pounds boneless skinless chicken thighs, cut into 1- to 2-inch pieces

3 tablespoons cornstarch

2¼ cups mochiko flour, divided

¼ cup sugar

6 garlic cloves, minced

1 tablespoon minced fresh ginger

1 teaspoon salt

¼ cup soy sauce

1 teaspoon sambal oelek

2 large eggs

Neutral oil, for frying

1½ cups all-purpose flour

FOR THE SPICY AIOLI

½ cup mayonnaise

1 tablespoon sriracha

1. **TO MAKE THE CHICKEN:** In a large glass bowl, combine the chicken, cornstarch, ¼ cup of mochiko flour, the sugar, garlic, ginger, salt, soy sauce, sambal oelek, and eggs and mix well. Cover and refrigerate for at least 3 hours or up to 24 hours for maximum flavor.

2. In a pot large enough to fry in, add at least 2 inches of oil, enough to submerge the chicken. Heat the oil to 375°F. To check if the oil is hot enough, add a peeled garlic clove to the oil. If the garlic starts bubbling and turns brown around the edges, the oil is ready for frying. Remove the garlic clove.

3. In a separate bowl, mix the all-purpose flour and remaining 2 cups of mochiko flour. Add the chicken one piece at a time and dredge in the flour mixture.

4. Slowly add the dredged chicken to the oil and fry for about 8 minutes, until crispy and golden brown and the center registers 165°F. Cook in batches as necessary.

5. Transfer the fried chicken to a paper towel–lined plate to drain the excess oil.

6. **TO MAKE THE SPICY AIOLI:** In a small bowl, whisk together the mayonnaise and sriracha. Serve alongside the chicken.

Ingredient Smarts: If you prefer a little more spice, add more sriracha or hot sauce to the aioli.

LEMON CHICKEN

Prep time: 15 minutes, plus 3 hours to marinate / **Cook time:** 30 minutes / **Serves 4 to 6**

This is the real deal: super crispy, extremely flavorful Lemon Chicken. It's a multistep process, but the result is totally worth it. The cornstarch in the marinade and breading creates a crispy and flaky coating that holds the fragrant sauce so well. If you know Lemon Chicken, you will love this recipe, and if you have never tried Lemon Chicken, you will also love this recipe!

FOR THE CHICKEN

5 large eggs

2 tablespoons sake

2 teaspoons salt

2 teaspoons garlic powder

1 teaspoon freshly ground black pepper

2¾ cups cornstarch, divided

4 pounds boneless, skin-on chicken thighs

Neutral oil, for frying

1½ cups all-purpose flour

1. **TO MAKE THE CHICKEN:** In a nonreactive bowl, combine the eggs, sake, salt, garlic powder, pepper, and ¾ cup of cornstarch and mix to combine. Add the chicken and let marinate for at least 3 hours in the refrigerator.

2. In a large pot, add 2 inches of oil, or enough to fully submerge the chicken. Heat the oil to 375°F. To check if the oil is hot enough, add a peeled garlic clove to the oil. If the garlic starts bubbling and turns brown around the edges, the oil is ready for frying. Remove the garlic clove.

3. In a separate bowl, add the flour and the remaining 2 cups of cornstarch. Add the chicken to the flour mixture and dredge each piece of chicken until it has a nice thick coating.

4. Slowly add the dredged chicken to the hot oil and fry for about 8 minutes, until crispy and golden brown and the center registers 165°F. Cook in batches as necessary.

5. Transfer the chicken to a paper towel–lined plate to drain the excess oil.

FOR THE LEMON SAUCE

2 cups water

½ cup white distilled vinegar

1 cup sugar

½ teaspoon salt

1 to 2 drops yellow food coloring (optional)

½ to 1 teaspoon lemon extract (taste after adding ½ teaspoon, and if you desire a sharper taste add the other ½ teaspoon)

5 lemon slices

3 tablespoons Cornstarch Slurry (page 102)

6. **TO MAKE THE LEMON SAUCE:** Meanwhile, in a small saucepan, combine the water, vinegar, sugar, salt, food coloring (if using), lemon extract, and lemon slices. Bring to a simmer.

7. Once simmering, slowly add the cornstarch slurry, adding a little at a time until it has a gravy-like consistency that is thick enough to coat the back of a spoon, about 5 minutes.

8. To serve, cut the chicken into strips and serve with the lemon sauce.

SHOYU PORK

5-INGREDIENT **ONE-POT**

Prep time: 10 minutes / **Cook time:** 45 minutes / **Serves 4**

This one-pot dish is super easy to make and always sells out at my restaurant. The sweet and salty flavor of the shoyu, sugar, and deep roasted sesame seeds penetrates the pork to yield tender meat that packs flavor in every bite. The resulting sauce is so delicious that you will be pouring it all over your rice, and that is totally okay (we won't judge you); we call that "gravy all over" here in the islands.

2½ pounds pork shoulder, cut into 1- to 2-inch cubes

4 cups Korean Barbecue Sauce (page 104)*

1 teaspoon sesame seeds

3 scallions, green parts only, for garnish

1. In a large pot, combine the pork shoulder with the Korean barbecue sauce, making sure the pork is fully submerged in the liquid. For the best flavor, soak the pork for at least 1 hour before cooking, but you can skip this step if you are in a rush.

2. Bring to a simmer over medium heat and cook, covered, for 20 minutes.

3. After 20 minutes of cooking, remove the cover and cook for another 20 minutes, or until the pork is fork-tender.

4. Garnish with the sesame seeds and scallions and serve.

*Shortcut: In a rush? Use a store-bought teriyaki sauce instead of the Korean barbecue sauce.

Make It a Combo: This dish is delicious over a hot bowl of rice with a bowl of cold Potato Mac Salad (page 21).

KALUA PIG AND CABBAGE

Prep time: 10 minutes / **Cook time:** 3 hours 5 minutes / **Serves 4**

Kalua Pig and Cabbage is the quintessential Hawaiian lū'au dish. The word "kalua" refers to the method of cooking in an underground oven. This traditional way of preparing the pork for a feast or lū'au produces the perfect salted, smoked morsels of meat, which trump everything on a local plate lunch, but this can be a time-consuming process. This stove-top recipe lets you recreate the flavors in a few hours, and most of the cooking is hands-off.

½ pork butt (about 3 pounds), cut into 3 large pieces

8 cups water

1½ tablespoons liquid smoke*

2 tablespoons salt, plus more for seasoning

½ head cabbage, cored and chopped into 1-inch chunks

1. In a large pot, combine the pork, water, liquid smoke, and 2 tablespoons of salt. Bring to a simmer over medium heat. Cover and cook for 2 to 3 hours, checking every ½ hour for doneness. You should be able to easily shred the meat.

2. Transfer the cooked pork to a bowl or pan, reserving at least 1 cup of the broth. Using two forks or two tongs, shred the pork into long strands, taste, and add more salt if needed. Set aside.

3. In a large pot, add the cabbage with 1 cup of the reserved broth. Cook for 5 minutes over medium heat, until the cabbage softens. Add in the shredded pork and serve.

*__Try This:__ You should be able to find liquid smoke at most supermarkets or online. Hickory flavored is best in this dish.

Ingredient Smarts: When cooking the kalua pig, make sure it is always covered with water.

CHICKEN LONG RICE

Prep time: 20 minutes, plus 1 hour 30 minutes to soak / **Cook time:** 1 hour / **Serves 4**

A classic Hawaiian comfort food, Chicken Long Rice is a Chinese-inspired noodle dish that is eaten at every lūʻau and pāʻina. In my house, my dad would make this for dinner quite often. I knew he was cooking it when I walked in the house and was hit with the distinct fragrance of ginger and chicken broth, and my day would instantly get better.

5 dried shiitake mushrooms

3 cups water

7 ounces bean thread noodles (saifun)*

½ yellow onion

3 tablespoons neutral oil

4 boneless, skinless chicken thighs, cut into 1-inch pieces

1 (3-inch) piece fresh ginger, lightly smashed

4 cups chicken broth

1 teaspoon salt

½ carrot, julienned

3 scallions, both green and white parts, cut into 2-inch pieces

Ingredient Smarts:
First blending the onions allows the flavor to really come through. If you can't find dried shiitake mushrooms, omit the mushrooms and use an extra cup of chicken broth instead.

1. In a small bowl, combine the mushrooms with the water and soak for 1 hour. Remove the mushrooms, reserving 1 cup of the soaking liquid, and slice the mushrooms lengthwise into strips, discarding the stems. Set aside.

2. In another bowl, soak the noodles for 30 minutes to allow them to rehydrate and soften. Drain and set aside.

3. In a food processor or blender, puree the onion.

4. In a large pot, heat the oil over medium-high heat. Add the chicken and cook until lightly browned. Add the pureed onion and sauté for 2 more minutes. Add the mushrooms, mushroom-soaking liquid, ginger, chicken broth, and salt. Simmer for 13 to 15 minutes, until the chicken is mostly cooked.

5. Add the noodles and carrot and simmer for 20 minutes longer, until the noodles are translucent, plump, and soft and the chicken is fork-tender.

6. Garnish with the scallions to serve. The longer you let it sit, the more broth the noodles will soak up. Waiting about 30 minutes to eat creates the perfect amount of noodle absorption.

*Try This: Look for these noodles in the Asian section of your supermarket or online. I like the Nice brand in the green package.

TERIYAKI CHICKEN

5-INGREDIENT

Prep time: 15 minutes, plus overnight to marinate / **Cook time:** 30 minutes / **Serves 4 to 6**

Whenever I eat a piece of grilled Teriyaki Chicken, I am instantly transported to birthday parties at the beach. Long family days at the beach or weekend camping trips always included some sweet and sticky Teriyaki Chicken grilled over a charcoal hibachi. This recipe uses an oven to cook the chicken, but feel free to grill the chicken if you have access to a grill.

4 pounds boneless, skin-on chicken thighs, butterflied

4 cups Teriyaki Sauce (page 105), divided*

3 tablespoons Cornstarch Slurry (page 102)

Make It a Combo:
Serve with Chili Pepper Water (page 98) and Somen Salad (page 78) to create the perfect summer (or anytime) plate.

1. Use paper towels to pat dry the chicken and remove any excess moisture. If using frozen chicken, make sure it is defrosted and patted dry, so you don't dilute the marinade.

2. Place the chicken in a gallon zip-top bag. Add 2 cups of teriyaki sauce to the bag, seal, and refrigerate for at least 24 hours to marinate.

3. In a medium saucepan over medium heat, add the remaining 2 cups of teriyaki sauce and bring to a simmer. Add the cornstarch slurry a little at a time while whisking continuously, until the sauce thickens and it can coat the back of a spoon.

4. Preheat the oven to 375°F and place the chicken skin-side up on a baking sheet. Bake for about 30 minutes, or until the chicken is cooked through and reaches an internal temperature of 165°F. If desired, you can transfer the chicken to a hot nonstick sauté pan skin-side down to crisp up the skin and give it some caramelization and color.

5. After the chicken is cooked, glaze with the thickened teriyaki sauce and enjoy.

*Shortcut:** Use store-bought teriyaki sauce to save time.

CHICKEN KATSU

Prep time: 15 minutes, plus 3 hours to marinate / **Cook time:** 20 minutes / **Serves 4 to 6**

If someone asked me for the perfect fried chicken, I think Chicken Katsu would have to be number one on the list. It is not your traditional battered chicken, but who decided buttermilk chicken was the "traditional" fried chicken anyway? This butterflied and panko-breaded chicken is light, packed with flavor, and truly a delicious meal for any occasion. Serve with Korean Barbecue Sauce (page 104), with Mushroom Onion Gravy (page 99) as a Loco Moco (page 50), or even as a spicy chicken sandwich—the possibilities are endless.

4 pounds boneless, skinless chicken thighs*

2 teaspoons salt

1 teaspoon freshly ground black pepper

1 teaspoon ground white pepper

2 teaspoons garlic powder

1½ teaspoons sesame oil

3 large eggs, beaten

2 tablespoons cornstarch

3 cups panko bread crumbs*

Neutral oil, for frying

4 cups cooked white rice

1½ cups Katsu Sauce (page 106)

1. Butterfly the chicken thighs so that the pieces are about ½ inch thick. You don't want thick pieces when you fry; if they are too thick, the panko will burn before the chicken cooks.

2. In a nonreactive bowl, add the chicken, salt, black and white peppers, garlic powder, sesame oil, eggs, and cornstarch and mix well. Marinate for at least 3 hours but preferably overnight.

3. Put the panko in a separate bowl or pan large enough so that the chicken pieces do not fold when laid inside.

4. To bread the chicken, use your non-dominant hand to pull a chicken piece out of the marinade and into the bowl with the panko. With your dominant hand, pat the chicken with panko. This will keep the panko from getting clumped up and keeps it on the chicken and not all over your hands. Repeat with the rest of the chicken pieces.

5. In a large pot, add at least 2 inches of oil to fully submerge the chicken. Heat the oil to 375°F. To check if the oil is hot enough, add a peeled garlic clove to the oil. If the garlic starts bubbling and turns brown around the edges, the oil is ready for frying. Remove the garlic clove.

6. Carefully add the panko-breaded chicken to the hot oil. Cook until golden and the chicken is cooked through and reaches an internal temperature of 165°F, taking care not to overcook. Set aside on a paper towel–lined plate to drain the excess oil.

7. Serve on a plate with rice and katsu sauce on the side or on a bun with Spicy Aioli (page 41) to make a spicy katsu sandwich.

*Try This: Feel free to use already butterflied chicken thighs or breasts, if available. You can find panko bread crumbs at most grocery stores, and any brand will do.

LOCO MOCO

Prep time: 10 minutes / **Cook time:** 15 minutes / **Serves 4**

One of my favorite Hawaiian comfort foods, Loco Moco is believed to have been invented on the Big Island, but I'm sure lots of people reading this from other islands will disagree. It is technically a breakfast item, but we eat it any time of the day. There are all types of Loco Mocos you can make, but it traditionally consists of two hamburger patties, rice, two over-easy eggs, and brown gravy.

2 white bread slices

2 tablespoons water

1½ pounds ground beef

9 large eggs, divided

2 teaspoons dried onion flakes

½ teaspoon garlic powder

1 teaspoon salt

½ teaspoon freshly ground black pepper

1 teaspoon ground white pepper (optional)

2 tablespoons neutral oil, divided

4 cups cooked white rice

2 cups Mushroom Onion Gravy (page 99)*

Make It a Combo: You can substitute Chicken Katsu (page 48) for the burger, or instead of gravy try using a Teriyaki Sauce (page 105) for a teriyaki loco moco.

1. In a large bowl, combine the bread and water. Mash using your hands to form a paste, adding more water if needed.

2. Add the ground beef to the mashed bread and mix. Add 1 egg, the onion flakes, garlic powder, salt, black pepper, and white pepper (if using) and mix well.

3. Using a ⅓-cup measuring cup, form the beef mixture into about 8 patties. Flatten the patties until they are about ½ inch thick. These burgers are not meant to be cooked rare because of the raw eggs. If you only have a grill, make the patties a little thicker.

4. In a nonstick pan or skillet, heat 1 tablespoon of oil over medium-high heat. Cook the hamburgers for 3 minutes on each side, allowing them to brown a bit.

5. In a separate nonstick pan, heat the remaining 1 tablespoon of oil over medium-high heat. Fry up the remaining 8 eggs in whichever style you prefer.

6. Put the rice at the bottom of each of four bowls and place a hamburger patty on top of the rice. Top each bowl with two eggs, warm gravy, and serve.

*Shortcut: If you don't have time to make your own gravy, feel free to use store-bought brown gravy.

HIBACHI BEACH PORK

Prep time: 10 minutes, plus overnight to marinate / **Cook time:** 20 minutes / **Serves 4 to 6**

This is more of a personal dish, because I'm not sure if anyone else in Hawai'i eats this. I just know that we made this all the time, and it would make our beach days so much tastier. My mom would rotate between chicken and pork, but both are fantastic. We use miso, beer, and peanut butter, and this sticky mess is full of flavor.

1 cup miso

1 cup brown sugar

½ cup creamy
  peanut butter

½ cup beer*

½ cup soy sauce

2 garlic cloves, minced

2 teaspoons minced or
  grated fresh ginger

3 pounds pork loin or
  boneless, skinless
  chicken thighs

Nonstick cooking spray

1. In a nonreactive bowl or zip-top bag, combine the miso, brown sugar, peanut butter, beer, soy sauce, garlic, and ginger. Add the pork and allow to marinate overnight.

2. Heat a grill, making sure to spray well with a nonstick spray. Take out the marinated meat, wiping off any excess marinade.

3. Cook the pork for 8 minutes per side on the grill, or until the internal temperature reaches 145°F.

4. Slice and serve.

*Try This:** For this recipe, light beers like lager or pale ale work best, rather than an IPA.

Cooking Tip: Serve with Portuguese Pickled Onions (page 24) to lighten the flavors of the miso and peanut butter.

ORANGE CHICKEN

Prep time: 15 minutes, plus 3 hours to marinate / **Cook time:** 30 minutes / **Serves 4**

Sweet, tangy, sticky, and crunchy are just a few adjectives to describe this Orange Chicken. This is my first choice to order at any restaurant that serves it. My dad's restaurant had a Chinese hot line (a line of food warming trays), and I would often sneak some orange chicken and hot mustard when no one was watching.

FOR THE CHICKEN

2 pounds boneless, skinless chicken thighs, cut into 1- to 2-inch pieces

½ teaspoon ground white pepper

½ teaspoon baking powder

1 teaspoon salt

1 teaspoon sesame oil

3 large eggs

Neutral oil, for frying

5 tablespoons cornstarch

3 tablespoons all-purpose flour

4 cups cooked white rice

1. **TO MAKE THE CHICKEN:** In a large nonreactive bowl, mix the chicken, white pepper, baking powder, salt, sesame oil, and eggs. Cover and marinate in the refrigerator for at least 3 hours, preferably overnight.

2. In a pot large enough to fry, add at least 2 inches of oil or enough to fully submerge the chicken. Heat the oil to 375°F. To check if the oil is hot enough, add a peeled garlic clove to the oil. If the garlic starts bubbling and turns brown around the edges, the oil is ready for frying. Remove the garlic clove.

3. Add the cornstarch and flour to the bowl with the marinated chicken and mix well.

4. Working in small batches, slowly add the chicken to the oil. Cook for about 8 minutes, until the internal temperature of the chicken reaches 165°F. Transfer the fried chicken to a paper towel–lined plate to drain the excess oil.

FOR THE ORANGE SAUCE

1½ cups sugar

1½ cups water

¼ cup soy sauce

¼ cup distilled white vinegar

2 garlic cloves, smashed

½ teaspoon salt

½ teaspoon ground white pepper

2 orange slices with rind

½ teaspoon sambal oelek

3 tablespoons Cornstarch Slurry (page 102)

5. **TO MAKE THE ORANGE SAUCE:** Meanwhile, in a medium sauce pot, combine the sugar, water, soy sauce, vinegar, garlic, salt, white pepper, orange slices, and sambal oelek. Bring to a simmer over medium-high heat.

6. Once the sauce is simmering, slowly add the cornstarch slurry a little at a time, until the sauce reaches a gravy-like consistency or thickens enough to coat the back of a spoon.

7. In a large bowl, toss the hot chicken with the thickened orange sauce. Enjoy over hot rice.

MOM'S CHINESE OXTAIL SOUP (LOCAL STYLE)

Prep time: 15 minutes / **Cook time:** 3 hours / **Serves 4 to 6**

This oxtail soup is my mom's recipe. The dried shiitake, star anise, tangerine peel, and peanuts all come together harmoniously to create layers of flavor. My mom is a fantastic cook, and we have dubbed her "soup goddess"; this winner of a dish justifies that name. There are many versions of oxtail soup, but this Chinese-style recipe recreates what you would mostly find on the islands. Serve with condiments and garnishes on the side with individual dipping bowls, so everyone can mix shoyu, grated ginger, and sambal oelek to their liking for dipping the oxtail.

12 to 14 dried shiitake mushrooms

3 cups water

3 to 4 pounds oxtail

1 gallon chicken or beef broth

3 thumb-size pieces fresh ginger, smashed

8 whole star anise

1 teaspoon whole black peppercorns

2 teaspoons salt

2 pieces chen pi (dried tangerine peel) *

1 cup raw or very lightly roasted peanuts, skin removed

1 mustard cabbage (kai choy), roughly chopped

½ cup chopped fresh cilantro, for garnish

8 scallions, green parts only, cut diagonally, for garnish

1. In a large bowl, soak the mushrooms in the water to rehydrate. When soft, remove from water and slice, discarding the hard stems and reserving the soaking liquid. Set aside.

2. Cut the excess fat off the oxtail. In a large pot, add the trimmed oxtail and cover with cold water. Bring to a boil over medium-high heat. When boiling, cook for 10 to 15 minutes and then discard the cooking water and rinse the oxtail.

3. Return the oxtail to a clean pot and add the broth to cover. If there is not enough broth, add water to cover. Add the ginger, star anise, peppercorns, salt, and chen pi. Simmer over medium-low heat, partially covered, for about 1 hour.

4. Add the soaked mushrooms, the reserved soaking liquid, and the peanuts. Continue to simmer, uncovered, for 1 to 1½ hours, until the oxtail is very tender. Skim the fat that rises to the top of the soup throughout the cooking process.

5. Add the mustard cabbage and cook until just limp.

6. Serve the oxtail soup in bowls and garnish with the cilantro and scallions.

*Try This: Tangerine peel (*chen pi*) can be found in most Asian stores or online. Alternatively, you can make your own in advance and store them in an airtight glass jar. Peel thin-skinned mandarins and scrape the white part out. String them together and hang in a sunny window with good airflow for a few weeks until perfectly dry. If you are in a hurry and don't have any chen pi available, substitute with strips of fresh orange zest.

Ingredient Smarts: This soup is even better the next day. It is very rich, like a bone broth, so it will "gel" overnight in the fridge. Just reheat slowly on the stove. If serving it the next day, add the mustard cabbage when ready to serve.

HAMBURGER STEAK

Prep time: 10 minutes / **Cook time:** 25 minutes / **Serves 4**

This Hamburger Steak recipe is moist and flavorful thanks to the raw egg. If you like thick, medium-rare hamburgers, then skip the egg and bread in the recipe and press out the patties as large as you want. If I could choose my last meal, I would choose this Hamburger Steak, but instead of gravy, I would use Teriyaki Sauce (page 105), for what we call "teri loco" on the islands.

2 white bread slices

2 tablespoons water

1½ pounds ground beef*

1 large egg

2 teaspoons dried onion flakes*

½ teaspoon garlic powder

1 teaspoon salt

½ teaspoon freshly ground black pepper

1 teaspoon ground white pepper (optional)

2 tablespoons neutral oil, divided

1 yellow onion, julienned

4 cups cooked white rice

3 cups Mushroom Onion Gravy (page 99)

1. In a large bowl, combine the bread and water. Mash to form a paste, adding more water if needed.

2. Add the ground beef to the mashed bread and mix to combine. Add the egg, onion flakes, garlic powder, salt, black pepper, and white pepper (if using) and mix well.

3. Using a ⅓-cup measuring cup, form the mixture into 8 patties. Smash patties until they are about ½ inch thick.

4. In a nonstick pan or skillet, add 1 tablespoon of the oil and the onion. Caramelize the onion slowly over medium-low heat for about 10 minutes. You can add 2 teaspoons of sugar to speed up the caramelization process. Once the onion is golden brown and sweet, remove from heat and set aside.

5. In a different nonstick pan, heat the remaining 1 tablespoon of oil over medium-high heat. Add the patties and cook through, about 3 minutes per side, until juicy and still soft. Do this in two batches if needed.

6. Serve two burger patties over 1 cup of white rice, topped with the mushroom onion gravy and caramelized onions.

*Try This: 80 percent lean/20 percent fat ground beef works well here. Look for dried onion flakes in the spice section of your supermarket.

Seared Ono with
Mango Salsa
PAGE 66

CHAPTER FOUR

Fish and Seafood

TEMPURA BATTERED MAHI-MAHI

5-INGREDIENT

Prep time: 15 minutes / **Cook time:** 30 minutes / **Serves 4**

Tempura batter can seem intimidating, but it really doesn't have to be. After all, the batter has only four ingredients. This light and airy batter can be used on other vegetables and seafood, so grab a few vegetables and enjoy a night of tempura with the family.

Tempura Batter (page 100)

1 tablespoon wasabi paste*

1 cup mayonnaise

4 cups neutral oil, for frying

1½ pounds mahi-mahi, cut into small fillets

Ingredient Smarts: If your batter isn't sticking to your fish or you want a thicker batter, simply dredge the fish in flour first then dip it into the batter. This is especially helpful when frying vegetables.

1. Make the tempura batter and set aside.

2. In a separate bowl, mix the wasabi and mayonnaise. Taste and add more wasabi if you like more spice. Set aside.

3. In a pot, add the oil and heat to 350°F. To check if the oil is hot enough, add a peeled garlic clove to the oil. If the garlic starts bubbling and turns brown around the edges, the oil is ready for frying. Remove the garlic clove.

4. Meanwhile, pat the mahi-mahi dry using paper towels. Dip one fillet into the batter and allow the excess to drip off.

5. Slowly add the battered fish to the hot oil, taking care not to drop it in to avoid sticking to the bottom of the pan.

6. Cook for about 4 minutes, until the mahi-mahi is golden brown, and serve with the wasabi aioli.

*Try This: Any brand of wasabi will do, and you can even use wasabi powder, but you must add water to it to form a paste.

COCONUT SHRIMP

Prep time: 15 minutes, plus 30 minutes to chill / **Cook time:** 20 minutes / **Serves 6**

Coconut Shrimp seems to be popular everywhere on the islands, and for good reason. We have ample coconut and the Kauai, Kahuku, and Kona shrimp are some of the tastiest in the world, so it makes sense that we would make a perfect Coconut Shrimp. This easy recipe will quickly become a family favorite.

1 large egg

1½ cups all-purpose flour, divided

½ cup soda water

1½ teaspoons baking powder

2 cups sweetened coconut flakes

25 shrimp, peeled, deveined, and butterflied

4 cups neutral oil, for frying

Ingredient Smarts: After rolling the shrimp in coconut flakes, it is very important that they chill in the refrigerator before frying. This allows the coconut to stick and will help prevent the coconut flakes from burning before the shrimp fully cooks. You can dredge the shrimp the day before, wrap well, freeze, and cook straight from frozen.

1. In a medium bowl, make the batter by combining the egg, ½ cup of flour, the soda water, and baking powder and mix well.

2. In a separate bowl, put the remaining 1 cup of flour. In another separate bowl, put the coconut flakes.

3. To dredge the shrimp, take one shrimp by the tail and dredge it in the flour, shaking off the excess. Dip the floured shrimp into the batter and allow the excess batter to drip off. Transfer the shrimp to the bowl with the coconut flakes and roll, until the shrimp is well coated. Transfer to a plate. Repeat with the rest of the shrimp. Transfer the plate of shrimp to the refrigerator and chill for at least 30 minutes.

4. In a large pot, heat the oil to 350°F. To check if the oil is hot enough, add a peeled garlic clove to the oil. When the garlic starts bubbling and turns brown around the edges, the oil is ready for frying. Remove the garlic clove.

5. Working in batches, carefully add the shrimp to the hot oil one at a time. Fry for about 3 minutes, until golden brown and fully cooked in the center.

MISO SALMON

Prep time: 10 minutes, plus overnight to marinate / **Cook time:** 10 minutes / **Serves 4**

Salmon may not be native to Hawai'i, but we sure do love it here! Miso Salmon and Teriyaki Salmon (page 65) are Island favorites. Even though I am not the biggest salmon fan, I love this recipe because the miso and sake bring so much flavor to this dish. Serve with pickled ginger.

1½ cups miso*
1½ cups brown sugar
½ cup sake
½ cup mirin
4 salmon fillets
Nonstick cooking spray

1. In a large bowl, mix the miso, brown sugar, sake, and mirin until well combined.

2. Add the salmon and let marinate overnight in the refrigerator.

3. Preheat the oven to broil. Line a baking sheet with aluminum foil and spray the foil with cooking spray.

4. Place the salmon skin-side down and broil for 5 to 10 minutes, or until the salmon is fully cooked. The color of the salmon will get very dark from the caramelization of all the sugar, but this is normal and adds amazing flavor.

*Try This: Preferably use white miso because it has a much milder and less salty flavor than its cousin, red miso.

Ingredient Smarts: You can use this same sauce and make delicious miso scallops, too. This is a quick and easy dish, but the prep is key. Marinate for a minimum of 24 hours for the best flavor.

NORI-CRUSTED MAHI-MAHI WITH WASABI AIOLI

5-INGREDIENT

Prep time: 5 minutes, plus 30 minutes to chill / **Cook time:** 10 minutes / **Serves 4**

Looking for something light and easy to make the family? This is it! The mahi-mahi can be substituted with any fish of your choosing, like salmon, ono, or ahi. Serve this over a bowl of rice such as "Whatever You Like" Fried Rice (page 29), soba noodles, or a fresh garden salad with the wasabi aioli on the side.

¼ cup furikake*

2 pounds fresh mahi-mahi or fish of your choice

1 tablespoon wasabi paste

1 cup mayonnaise

2 tablespoons melted butter

1. Pour the furikake seasoning onto a plate.

2. Press the fish into the furikake and place in the refrigerator for 30 minutes.

3. Meanwhile, in a separate bowl, combine the wasabi and mayonnaise and mix until combined. Taste and add more wasabi as needed.

4. In a nonstick pan or skillet, heat the butter over medium heat and cook the mahi-mahi for 3 minutes on each side for medium-rare, or cook more until it reaches your desired doneness. Serve with a generous drizzle of the wasabi aioli.

*Try This: If you can't find furikake, you can make your own by grinding 3 nori sheets with 1 tablespoon of sesame seeds and adding salt to taste.

POKE BOWL

QUICK

Prep time: 20 minutes / **Serves 4**

Poke has become increasingly trendy, with poke places popping up all over the world, even in land-locked states and countries. Poke is about simplicity, and the original Hawaiian poke was just fish, sea salt, inamona (ground kukui nut), and limu (seaweed). Now we have many versions featuring crab, octopus, cucumber, and much more. This tuna poke is the perfect balance of salty and sweet. Feel free to make it your own with your favorite ingredients. If you like spicy, add a ½ teaspoon of sambal oelek.

2 pounds fresh ahi tuna, cut into 1-inch cubes*

Pinch salt

1 garlic clove, minced

2 teaspoons minced fresh ginger

3 tablespoons low-sodium soy sauce

1 tablespoon sugar

1 teaspoon sesame oil

2 scallions, green parts only, cut diagonally

4 cups cooked white rice

½ avocado, chopped into cubes

2 teaspoons furikake

1. In a large bowl, combine the tuna with a generous pinch of salt. Mix and allow to sit for at least 10 minutes.

2. In a separate bowl, mix the garlic, ginger, soy sauce, sugar, sesame oil, and scallions.

3. Pour the garlic mixture over the tuna and mix well.

4. Serve each portion of tuna over 1 cup of rice. Top with the avocado and furikake.

*Try This: Feel free to substitute the tuna with medium-firm tofu or any other sashimi-grade seafood.

Ingredient Smarts: One of the things that I like to do with my fish before marinating it is lay it out on a plate or pan and salt it. Properly seasoning the fish creates better flavor.

TERIYAKI SALMON

5-INGREDIENT

Prep time: 20 minutes / **Cook time:** 15 minutes / **Serves 4**

Every time I put a teriyaki grilled salmon bowl on the specials board at my restaurant, it always sells out before dinner. This sauce truly brings the salmon to a whole new level! Salmon is known as a forgiving fish because of its oil and fat content, which makes this dish even easier to cook. Whether you grill or roast this salmon, I guarantee it is not going to be your normal boring salmon fillet.

---

3 cups Teriyaki Sauce (page 105)

3 tablespoons Cornstarch Slurry (page 102)

Nonstick cooking spray

4 salmon fillets

4 cups cooked white rice

Cooking Tip: To grill the salmon, get a grill very hot and spray with some nonstick spray. Place the salmon skin-side down and allow to cook for about 3 minutes. Flip, brush on the teriyaki sauce, and close the lid to allow it to cook for another 3 to 5 minutes, or until the salmon is cooked to your liking and the sauce is nice and sticky.

1. In a nonreactive pot, bring the teriyaki sauce to a simmer over medium-high heat.

2. In a small bowl, mix the cornstarch and water well. Slowly add the cornstarch slurry to the simmering teriyaki sauce and whisk until thickened. Cook for an additional 3 minutes and remove from heat. Set aside.

3. Preheat the oven to broil. Line a baking sheet with aluminum foil and spray the foil with cooking spray.

4. Place the salmon skin-side down and broil for about 5 minutes. Generously glaze the salmon with the teriyaki glaze and finish broiling for 5 more minutes, until the glaze is nice and caramelized and the salmon is cooked to your liking.

5. After the salmon is finished cooking, transfer to a plate and add a little more teriyaki glaze. Serve it in a bowl over rice.

---

*Shortcut: Use a store-bought teriyaki sauce if desired.

SEARED ONO WITH MANGO SALSA

Prep time: 15 minutes / **Cook time:** 10 minutes / **Serves 4**

Mango and pineapple salsa is everywhere on the islands, not because salsa is native to Hawai'i but because of our abundance of the world's best mangos and pineapples. And when the world gives you mangos, why not make salsa? For this dish, any white fish will do, or even a seared ahi would work beautifully.

1 cup chopped
fresh mango*

½ cucumber, seeded
and chopped

½ red bell pepper,
chopped

¼ cup minced red onion

1 tablespoon chopped
fresh cilantro (optional)

1 jalapeño, seeded
and minced

3 tablespoons freshly
squeezed lime juice

½ tablespoon neutral oil

4 to 6 ono or mahi-mahi
fillets (about 2 pounds)

Salt

1. In a bowl, combine the mango, cucumber, bell pepper, onion, cilantro (if using), jalapeño, and lime juice. Mix and refrigerate for at least 15 minutes.

2. In a nonstick pan, heat the oil over medium-high heat. Season the ono with salt and sear for about 3 minutes on each side, until cooked.

3. Serve by placing the cooked fish on a plate and a heaping spoonful of salsa on top.

*Try This: If you can't find fresh mango, you can use fresh peaches or frozen mango, or use canned pineapple tidbits instead and cut them up a bit.

SALT AND PEPPER SHRIMP

Prep time: 15 minutes / **Cook time:** 20 minutes / **Serves 4**

Salt and Pepper Shrimp gets its name from the key ingredients, but the pepper used is not cracked black pepper but Szechuan peppercorns. The Szechuan peppercorns gives the dish a "numbing" sensation, and the simple flavors will have you coming back for more.

2 teaspoons Szechuan peppercorns*

1 tablespoon salt

25 shrimp, shell on and deveined

3 tablespoons cornstarch

1 tablespoon neutral oil, plus more for frying

2 teaspoons chopped fresh ginger

3 garlic cloves, minced

1 red chile pepper, chopped

3 scallions, both green and white parts, cut diagonally

Ingredient Smarts:
When toasting and grinding the peppercorns and salt, you can use a food processor. It is easier to grind if you do a bigger batch, and you can put the salt and pepper mixture into a mason jar and store for up to 1 month.

1. In a pan, slowly toast the peppercorns and salt over medium heat for about 5 minutes, until the salt starts to turn a very light yellow.

2. Transfer the toasted peppercorn mix to a spice grinder or food processor and grind to a powder. Set aside.

3. Pat the shrimp dry and dredge in the cornstarch. Shake to let the excess cornstarch fall off.

4. Add about 3 inches of oil to a pot, enough to cover the shrimp. Heat the oil to 350°F. To check if the oil is hot enough, add a peeled garlic clove to the oil. When the garlic starts bubbling and turns brown around the edges, the oil is ready for frying. Remove the garlic clove.

5. Carefully add the shrimp to the hot oil. Deep fry for about 2 minutes, remove, and place on a paper towel–lined plate.

6. In a clean nonstick pan, heat the remaining 1 tablespoon of oil over medium-high heat. Add the ginger, garlic, chile pepper, and scallions and quickly stir-fry for a few seconds until cooked but not brown.

7. Add the shrimp and about three-quarters of the pepper and salt mixture. Toss well and transfer to a serving plate.

*Try This: You can easily find Szechuan peppercorns online or in any Asian market; if not, try using black or pink peppercorns, but cut down the pepper by half. You won't experience the numbing effect, but it will still taste great.

SPICY CRAB AND RICE PARTY PAN

QUICK

Prep time: 10 minutes / **Cook time:** 5 minutes / **Serves 4 to 6**

Showing up to a party with a spicy crab pan and a pack full of nori sheets instantly makes you the life of the party! I call it "Hawaiian lasagna." This dish is a layer of sushi rice seasonsed with furikake, covered by a thick layer of spicy crab, and lightly broiled in the oven. Serve this with some nori and a spoon, allowing people to scoop a little of everything and eat it with the nori like you would a lettuce wrap.

¼ cup rice vinegar

½ cup sugar

1 tablespoon salt, plus more for seasoning

4 cups cooked white short-grain rice

Nonstick cooking spray

1 (16-ounce) can imitation crab

½ cup mayonnaise

1 tablespoon sriracha

¼ cup furikake

1 package toasted salted nori sheets*

1. In a small saucepan over low heat, heat the vinegar, sugar, and salt until the sugar is melted. Remove from the heat and allow the mixture to cool to room temperature.

2. Place the white rice in a large bowl. Gently fan the rice while slowly adding the vinegar and sugar mixture, a little at a time, and folding it into the rice. Repeat this process until the vinegar and sugar mixture is completely used.

3. Preheat the oven to broil. Spray a 9-by-13-inch pan with cooking spray.

4. In a separate bowl, combine the imitation crab, mayonnaise, and sriracha. Add salt to taste.

5. Add the rice to the pan and spread it out in an even layer. Season generously with the furikake. Add the crab mixture on top of the rice and spread it out into an even layer.

6. Transfer the pan to the oven and broil until the top just starts to brown.

7. Serve with the nori sheets and a serving spoon.

***Try This:** Nori sheets comes in precut versions, but if you get the larger sheets, just cut each sheet into four equal pieces.*

GARLIC SHRIMP

Prep time: 10 minutes, plus 1 hour to marinate / **Cook time:** 20 minutes / **Serves 4**

The popular Hawaiian shrimp trucks are one of the more recent food phenomena to take over the islands. They were created on Oahu to promote the Kahuku shrimp farms and have become extremely popular for very delicious reasons. This simple dish will transport you right to the beautiful North Shore of Oahu. Serve over white rice or with dinner rolls like Portuguese sweet bread.

FOR THE MARINADE

2 tablespoons chopped garlic

1 tablespoon paprika

1 teaspoon kosher salt

½ cup olive oil*

Juice of ½ lemon

FOR THE SHRIMP

1 pound shrimp, shell on and deveined

1 cup cornstarch

¼ cup all-purpose flour

2 tablespoons neutral oil, divided

5 tablespoons unsalted butter

¼ cup chopped garlic

Juice of ½ lemon

Salt

Ingredient Smarts: Keep the shell on to make the shrimp crispy on the outside and moist and sweet on the inside. If you don't want the shells, marinate per instructions, but skip the flour and cornstarch in step 3.

1. **TO MAKE THE MARINADE:** In a zip-top bag or glass bowl, combine the garlic, paprika, salt, olive oil, and lemon juice. Add the shrimp and toss to mix. Marinate for at least 1 hour.

2. **TO MAKE THE SHRIMP:** In a large bowl, combine the cornstarch and flour and mix well.

3. Add the shrimp to the cornstarch and flour mixture. Dredge the shrimp, shaking off the excess flour.

4. In a nonstick pan, heat 1 tablespoon of oil over medium-high heat.

5. Cooking in batches, add the shrimp and cook for about 3 minutes on each side, until the shells are crispy. Transfer the cooked shrimp to a paper towel–lined plate. Pour the fry oil out of the pan.

6. In the same pan over medium heat, melt the butter and remaining 1 tablespoon of oil. When hot, add the garlic. Cook until fragrant, about 30 seconds. Do not allow it to burn.

7. Return the shrimp to the pan. Cook for 3 to 5 minutes, until the garlic is just caramelized. Add the lemon juice and salt to taste.

*Try This: Make sure the olive oil is not extra-virgin. You can also use any other oil with a higher smoking point, like avocado.

Somen Salad
PAGE 78

CHAPTER FIVE

Plant-Based

SESAME NOODLE SALAD

Prep time: 15 minutes / **Cook time:** 15 minutes / **Serves 4**

In Chinese culture, a long noodle symbolizes a long life or yi mein. Who doesn't want a long life, right? The crunch from the snap peas and cucumbers, along with the sweetness of the peppers, acid from the citrus, and the creamy peanut butter–sesame dressing, makes this noodle salad a delicious addition to your quest for a long life.

FOR THE SALAD

4 ounces vermicelli (thin spaghetti)

1 pound Chinese snow peas or sugar snap peas, strings removed

Salt

1 cucumber, seeded and julienned into 2-inch sticks

1 red bell pepper, julienned in 1- to 2-inch sticks

3 scallions, both green and white parts, cut diagonally

1 tablespoon chopped fresh cilantro

Freshly ground black pepper

1. **TO MAKE THE SALAD:** Cook the pasta according to box instructions. Drain and rinse the pasta. Set aside to cool and dry completely.

2. Lightly salt a pot of water and bring to a boil over high heat. Quickly blanch the peas for about 2 minutes.

3. Drain and cool the peas in a bowl with water and ice. Once cool, remove and set aside.

4. **TO MAKE THE DRESSING:** In a food processor or blender, add the peanut butter, vinegar, soy sauce, sesame oil, honey, garlic, ginger, and lemon juice and process until smooth. Transfer the dressing to a bowl and slowly whisk in the oil.

5. In a salad bowl, combine the noodles and half of the dressing and toss to coat the noodles evenly with the dressing.

FOR THE DRESSING

½ cup peanut butter

¼ cup rice vinegar

5 tablespoons soy sauce

3 tablespoons sesame oil

2 tablespoons honey

2 garlic cloves, peeled

2 teaspoons minced
   fresh ginger

Juice of 1 lemon

1 cup neutral oil

6. Add the peas, cucumber, bell pepper, scallions, cilantro, and the second half of the dressing to the bowl with the noodles and lightly toss. Taste and season with salt and pepper if needed.

Ingredient Smarts: Drying the pasta allows the dressing to better coat it. I like to put it in the refrigerator to help the drying process.

VEGETABLE TEMPURA

Prep time: 20 minutes / **Cook time:** 20 minutes / **Serves 4**

Tempura is a dish that can go two ways. The first is a beautifully choreographed dance that ends up with minimal mess and a light, crispy tempura batter. The other gets you the same results, only you are left with a kitchen that looks like a batter hurricane blew through it. Keep organized when preparing this recipe. Have your vegetables cut, your bowls separated, and a nice deep pot filled just halfway with oil to prevent splatter.

Tempura Batter (page 100)

4 cups neutral oil, for frying

1 cup all-purpose flour

1 cup water

1 zucchini, cut into ½-inch rounds

1 (8-ounce) package button mushrooms

½ sweet onion, cut into ½-inch rounds (like onion rings) *

Salt

1 cup Bug Juice (page 101)

Cooking Tip: To check if the oil is hot enough for frying, add a peeled garlic clove to the oil. If the garlic starts bubbling and turns brown around the edges, the oil is ready. Remove the garlic clove.

1. Make the tempura batter and set aside.

2. In a large pot, heat the oil to 350°F (see cooking tip).

3. In one bowl, place the flour for dredging, and in another bowl, place the water.

4. Dip the vegetables in the water one piece at a time, allowing any excess to drip off, until the vegetables are just a little wet enough for the flour to stick to them.

5. Dredge the wet vegetables in the flour, shaking off the excess. Finally, slowly dip the floured vegetables into the tempura batter, allowing the excess to drip off.

6. Fry in the hot oil until golden brown, about 2 to 5 minutes, depening on the type of vegetable. Transfer to a paper towel–lined plate to drain the oil.

7. Sprinkle with a little salt. Serve with the bug juice.

*Try This: If you can find them, Maui onions are great here, but yellow onion is okay to substitute as well.

EGG FOO YOUNG

Prep time: 15 minutes / **Cook time:** 20 minutes / **Serves 4**

If you are at any good Chinese restaurant in Hawai'i, you will probably find Egg Foo Young. This is my version of the classic and, if done right, is very close to what you would find in a restaurant. My vegetarian version is filled with cabbage, carrot, and onion and seasoned with toasted sesame oil. This Egg Foo Young just might replace your favorite Denver omelet.

½ head cabbage, shredded

½ carrot, shredded

1 yellow onion, julienned

1 teaspoon sesame oil

½ teaspoon ground white pepper

Pinch salt

Freshly ground black pepper

6 large eggs

1 tablespoon neutral oil

1. Fill a large pot with salted water and bring to a boil. Blanch the cabbage, carrot, and onion. You want the vegetables to have a bite to them, so just a quick blanch of about 2 minutes is enough. Rinse with cold water and let drain completely. Using a colander, press down on the vegetables to squeeze out any excess water.

2. In a large bowl, combine the cooled and drained vegetables and add the sesame oil, white pepper, salt, and black pepper to taste. Mix to combine.

3. Add the eggs into the vegetable mixture and mix until combined.

4. In a nonstick pan, heat the oil over medium-high heat.

5. Using a ladle, add the egg and vegetable mixture into the pan to form a flat pancake shape. Cook on each side for about 4 minutes, until the egg is fully cooked.

Ingredient Smarts: Blanching the vegetables allows for more even cooking. If you like your vegetables less cooked and still crunchy, feel free to skip the blanching in step 1.

GRILLED TERIYAKI TOFU WITH GARLIC-CHILI OIL

Prep time: 10 minutes, plus 3 hours to marinate / **Cook time:** 20 minutes / **Serves 4**

How delicious can a block of tofu really be? This was my mentality until I tried grilled tofu smothered in crunchy garlic-chili oil. Don't be intimidated by the chili oil process because, once you make your first batch, it will go a long way.

2 (16-ounce) packs medium-firm or firm tofu

3 cups Korean Barbecue Sauce (page 104), divided*

3 tablespoons Cornstarch Slurry (page 102)

Nonstick cooking spray

2 cups Garlic-Chili Oil Crunch (page 103)*

1 tablespoon grated fresh ginger

½ cup grated daikon*

2 scallions, both white and green parts, cut diagonally

Make It a Combo: Serve with my "Whatever You Like" Fried Rice (page 29) and Namasu (page 25) or Takuwan (page 20).

1. In a large bowl, soak the tofu in 2 cups of Korean barbecue sauce for at least 3 hours and up to overnight.

2. Get a grill very hot and preheat the oven to 400°F.

3. In a small saucepan over medium-high heat, bring the remaining 1 cup of Korean barbecue sauce to a boil. Slowly add the cornstarch slurry to create a thick glaze. Set aside.

4. Spray the grill with cooking spray and quickly grill the tofu blocks to give them nice grill marks.

5. Transfer to a pan and rub Korean glaze all over the tops of the tofu blocks and cook in the oven for about 3 minutes, or until the glaze starts to caramelize.

6. Serve with the garlic-chili oil, grated ginger, grated daikon, and scallions.

*Shortcut: Use premade store-bought teriyaki sauce and chili oil in a pinch.

*Try This: If you can't find daikon, you can use red radishes instead, but they will be a bit spicier.

Cooking Tip: Making sure the grill is extremely hot is very important. I like to spray the grill and lightly spray the tofu to ensure there is no sticking and very deep grill marks.

TARO AND CORN CHOWDER

ONE-POT

Prep time: 15 minutes / **Cook time:** 40 minutes / **Serves 4**

This was one of my dad's most popular soup specials at his Hawaiian restaurant. Every time someone would bring him a taro or 'ulu (breadfruit), he would make this soup and it would always sell out by dinner. Feel free to substitute coconut milk instead of milk and cream for a dairy-free option.

1 tablespoon neutral oil

1 onion, minced

1 celery stalk, minced

2 tablespoons butter

5 garlic cloves, minced

2 tablespoons all-purpose flour

3 cups vegetable broth

1 cup heavy (whipping) cream

1 cup milk

1 large taro root, peeled and cut into 1- to 2-inch chunks*

2 sweet potatoes, peeled and cut into 1- to 2-inch chunks

2 cups frozen corn

2 teaspoons Worcester-shire sauce

Salt

Freshly ground black pepper

1. In a large pot, heat the oil over medium heat. Sauté the onion and celery for about 3 minutes, until translucent. Add the butter and garlic and cook until the butter is melted.

2. Add the flour and stir until the mixture thickens into a paste (roux). Cook for 2 minutes, stirring continuously.

3. Add the vegetable broth, cream, and milk and bring to a simmer.

4. Add the taro and cook for 20 minutes, or until tender. Add the sweet potatoes and cook for an additional 15 minutes, until the sweet potato is soft and the chowder has thickened.

5. Add the corn and Worcestershire and heat through. Season with salt and pepper to taste.

*Try This: Use 3 russet potatoes if taro is unavailable.

Ingredient Smarts: I love to add 2 teaspoons of apple cider vinegar after the soup is finished. It adds a tiny bit of balance and gives the soup a beautiful shine.

SOMEN SALAD

QUICK

Prep time: 15 minutes / **Cook time:** 15 minutes / **Serves 4**

Somen Salad is probably our second-most popular cold noodle salad here in Hawai'i (if you consider macaroni "noodles"). It is a popular potluck dish because it is composed on one platter, looks beautiful, and everyone loves it. Traditionally, chicken broth is used for this dish, but this version uses vegetable broth.

FOR THE DRESSING

1 cup vegetable broth

¼ cup soy sauce

¼ cup sugar

1 tablespoon sesame oil

FOR THE SALAD

1 (12-ounce) pack dried somen noodles

1 tablespoon neutral oil

2 large eggs, whipped

½ head napa cabbage, shredded

2 scallions, both green and white parts, cut diagonally

3 ounces kamaboko (fishcake)*

1 Japanese cucumber, seeded and julienned into 2-inch sticks

1 carrot, julienned or shaved

1 yellow and/or red bell pepper, julienned

1. **TO MAKE THE DRESSING:** In a bowl, combine the broth, soy sauce, sugar, and sesame oil and whisk until the sugar is dissolved.

2. **TO MAKE THE SALAD:** In a large pot, cook the somen noodles according to package instructions. Drain, rinse, and transfer to the refrigerator to cool.

3. In a nonstick pan, heat the oil over medium-high heat and add the eggs to the pan. Rotate the pan so that the egg can spread out as much as possible. Cook for 2 minutes on each side, until cooked through. Transfer to a cutting board and slice into four pieces.

4. Put the noodles on a large serving tray or pan. Arrange rows of cabbage, scallions, kamaboko, cucumber, egg strips, carrot, and bell pepper on top of the noodles.

5. Serve with the dressing in a condiment container, so everyone can dress their salads individually. The dressing will last for up to 2 weeks in the refrigerator.

*Try This: Kamaboko, also called fishcake, can be found in most Asian markets, but if you don't have any, you can add some baby bay shrimp or crab. Or leave it out completely and replace it with any of your favorite vegetables.

COCONUT CURRY STEW

Prep time: 20 minutes / **Cook time:** 30 minutes / **Serves 4 to 6**

Coconut curry is a house favorite. The best part about this dish is its versatility. If you wanted to add shrimp you could; if you want to make a red curry instead of green, just swap out the different curry paste. I also love chopping up a fresh pineapple and garnishing the curry with it to create a level of flavor that no one is expecting.

1 tablespoon neutral oil

½ onion, chopped

1 carrot, cut into 1-inch cubes

1 (14-ounce) can coconut milk

3 tablespoons green curry paste

1 cup vegetable broth

3 makrut lime leaves (optional)

3 teaspoons sugar

1 russet potato, cut into ½-inch cubes

2 Japanese eggplants or 1 English eggplant, cut into 1-inch cubes

Salt

10 Thai basil leaves, chopped

Squeeze fresh lime juice

1. In a large pot, heat the oil over medium-high heat. Add the onion and carrot and sauté for 3 minutes, or until the onions are translucent.

2. Add the coconut milk and green curry paste. Mix well and bring to a simmer.

3. Add the vegetable broth, lime leaves (if using), and sugar and bring back up to a simmer.

4. When gently simmering, add the potato and cook for about 20 minutes, or until the potato is just about soft. Add the eggplant and cook for 10 to 15 minutes, until tender. Season with salt to taste.

5. Serve with Thai basil and a squeeze of lime juice.

EGGPLANT STIR-FRY

Prep time: 20 minutes, plus 1 hour to rest / **Cook time:** 20 minutes / **Serves 4**

This will quickly become your family's new favorite. The soft, sweet eggplant with this extremely aromatic sauce is the perfect combination. Although this dish takes a little more attention and focus to prepare, it is all worth it in the end when you take that first bite.

FOR THE SAUCE

1 tablespoon light soy sauce*

1 tablespoon water

1 tablespoon oyster sauce

2 teaspoons sugar

1 teaspoon cornstarch

FOR THE EGGPLANT

3 Japanese eggplant, chopped into diagonal 1-inch pieces

1½ teaspoons kosher salt

1 tablespoon cornstarch

3 tablespoons neutral oil, divided

4 garlic cloves, minced

1 teaspoon minced fresh ginger

3 tablespoons toasted peanuts

2 scallions, both green and white parts, cut diagonally

1. **TO MAKE THE SAUCE:** In a small bowl, combine the soy sauce, water, oyster sauce, sugar, and cornstarch and mix well. Set aside.

2. **TO MAKE THE EGGPLANT:** Spread the eggplant on a plate or pan lined with paper towels and sprinkle with the salt on both sides. Let sit for at least 1 hour. Pat dry but do not rinse.

3. Toss the salted eggplant in the cornstarch until lightly dusted, shaking off the excess.

4. In a large nonstick pan, heat 2 tablespoons of the oil over medium-high heat. Add a layer of eggplant to the pan and cook for about 10 minutes total, until golden brown on each side, then transfer to a plate.

5. In a clean nonstick pan, add the remaining 1 tablespoon of oil, the garlic, and ginger and sauté for 3 minutes over medium heat, until fragrant.

6. Pour the sauce into the pan and simmer for 3 minutes, until thickened.

7. As soon as it thickens, add the eggplant to the pan and toss, allowing sauce to coat the eggplant evenly.

8. Garnish with the peanuts and scallions to serve.

*Try This: If you don't have light soy sauce, regular soy sauce (shoyu) can be used.

Make It a Combo: Add some tofu to this dish and serve with brown rice or cauliflower rice for a delicious low-fat meal for the whole family to enjoy.

Ingredient Smarts: Do not skip the salting process. This helps draw the moisture from the eggplant and will prevent it from becoming saturated in oil and ripping apart.

TOFU LETTUCE WRAPS

QUICK

Prep time: 15 minutes / **Serves 4 to 6**

I created these lettuce wraps originally as mahi-mahi ceviche lettuce wraps (and that is still a delicious option); however, the one time that I made a vegetarian version using fresh local Hilo tofu, everyone at the party ate the vegetarian version and we ended up making the switch permanent. This is also delicious served with a Thai peanut sauce as an accompaniment.

FOR THE SAUCE

1 garlic clove, minced

2 teaspoons minced fresh ginger

3 tablespoons soy sauce

1 tablespoon sugar

1 teaspoon sesame oil

2 scallions, green parts only, roughly chopped

FOR THE WRAPS

1 (16-ounce) package medium-firm or firm tofu

Salt

3 heads butter lettuce, separated*

¼ cup chopped honey roasted peanuts

1 carrot, julienned or shredded

½ bunch cilantro

1 cucumber, halved lengthwise, seeded, and julienned

1. **TO MAKE THE SAUCE:** In a small bowl, combine the garlic, ginger, soy sauce, sugar, sesame oil, and scallions. Whisk the sauce well and set aside.

2. **TO MAKE THE WRAPS:** Place the tofu in a large bowl. Using your hand or a fork, lightly mash the tofu until the consistency resembles ground meat.

3. Add the sauce to the bowl with the tofu, toss to coat, and season with salt to taste.

4. Serve the tofu in a bowl in the center of a serving platter, surrounded by lettuce leaves and the peanuts, carrot, cilantro, and cucumber.

*Try This: You can use green leaf or any soft leaf lettuce instead of butter lettuce.

Banana Cream Parfait
PAGE 93

CHAPTER SIX

Snacks and Desserts

HURRICANE POPCORN

5-INGREDIENT   QUICK

Prep time: 5 minutes / **Cook time:** 5 minutes / **Makes 5 cups**

If you ever lived in Hawai'i or live with someone who has lived in Hawai'i, chances are you have eaten a form of Hurricane Popcorn! Whenever I go to the movies and get my popcorn, if there is no kakimochi (Japanese rice crackers) then I won't eat it. Ditch the messy melted M&Ms and try some Hurricane Popcorn next time you and your family have a movie night.

¼ cup salted butter*

5 cups popped popcorn

1 cup kakimochi (Japanese rice crackers)*

⅓ cup furikake*

1. In a small saucepan over medium heat, melt the butter. When the butter starts to bubble and foam, immediately reduce the heat to low and cook for about 3 minutes.

2. When little brown bits start forming on the bottom, strain or ladle only the top layer of the butter, discarding the little brown bits and fats. This top pure layer is the clarified butter.

3. In a bowl, combine the popcorn with the clarified butter, kakimochi, and furikake. Serve immediately.

*Try This: Kakimochi, also known as arare, can be found at most Asian markets or online. Look for Tomoe Brand and Asian Trans. For the furikake, try to get the plain furikake, also called nori komi furikake.

*Shortcut: If you don't want to make your own clarified butter, use store-bought ghee.

MACADAMIA NUT AND WHITE CHOCOLATE CHIP COOKIES

QUICK

Prep time: 10 minutes / **Cook time:** 10 minutes / **Makes about 10 cookies**

The first business that I ever opened was a coffee and pastry shop with my wife, who made all our desserts. Her cookies were literally the size of people's faces, and their flavor was just as big. I loved the touch of sea salt that she would add, and I believe it was what kept people coming back for more.

Nonstick cooking spray

1 cup (2 sticks) butter, melted

1 cup brown sugar

½ cup granulated white sugar

½ tablespoon vanilla extract

1 large egg

1 large egg yolk

2 cups all-purpose flour

½ teaspoon salt

½ teaspoon baking soda

1 cup white chocolate chips

¼ cup chopped macadamia nuts

Sea salt

1. Preheat the oven to 375°F. Spray a baking sheet with cooking spray.

2. In a mixer, combine the butter, brown sugar, white sugar, vanilla, whole egg, and egg yolk and mix until smooth.

3. In a separate bowl, combine the flour, salt, and baking soda and mix well.

4. Add the dry ingredients to the wet ingredients and mix until incorporated.

5. Fold in the chocolate chips and macadamia nuts until evenly distributed.

6. Scoop about ¼ cup of dough onto the prepared baking sheet for each cookie, leaving at least 2 inches between the cookies. Sprinkle the cookies with a pinch of sea salt.

7. Bake for 8 to 10 minutes, or until the cookies start to get a little golden but are still soft in the center. Do not overbake.

8. Remove from the oven and allow to cool before serving.

PINEAPPLE WHIP

5-INGREDIENT   QUICK

Prep time: 20 minutes / **Serves 4**

Pineapple Whip was first served at the Dole plantation and has now become famous worldwide and is served at theme parks everywhere. This three-ingredient, super easy recipe is perfect for a hot summer day.

4 cups frozen
    pineapple chunks

1 cup coconut milk*

1 teaspoon freshly
    squeezed lime juice

1. In a blender, combine the frozen pineapple, coconut milk, and lime juice and blend until smooth.

2. Enjoy immediately.

*Try This: You can replace the coconut milk with almond milk or any milk of your choice.

Ingredient Smarts: This dessert is very easy to make, but the key is to make sure the pineapple is frozen solid for the best texture.

ICE CAKE

5-INGREDIENT   ONE-POT

Prep time: 5 minutes, plus 2 hours to freeze / **Serves 4**

I always had a sweet tooth, and Ice Cakes always helped satisfy that craving. This super easy recipe is a play on what I grew up eating out of the plastic cups with a wooden flat spoon at my grandma's house in Hilo. It is like a hybrid between ice cream, shaved ice, and an ice pop. My favorite part of this recipe is that you can substitute any soda instead of strawberry, like pineapple, grape, or orange; the possibilities are endless (well, based on what soda the grocery store has)!

½ cup sweetened condensed milk

2 tablespoons heavy (whipping) cream

6 ounces lemon-lime soda

12 ounces strawberry-flavored soda

1. In a bowl, combine the condensed milk and cream and mix well.

2. Add the sodas. Lightly mix until just incorporated, leaving air bubbles intact.

3. Ladle the milk and soda mixture into 6-ounce plastic cups and place in the freezer. Allow to freeze for at least 2 hours.

Ingredient Smarts: Do not overmix in step 2. Keeping the light, airy bubbles from the carbonation intact is key to making a good Ice Cake.

HAUPIA PIE

Prep time: 10 minutes, plus 2 hours 40 minutes to chill / **Cook time:** 15 minutes

Serves 4 to 6

Haupia can be compared to Italian panna cotta or a firmer version of Mexican flan. It's an easy, cheap, creamy custard dessert that was probably created because of the abundance of sugar and coconuts here on the islands. This version includes a crust of Oreo cookie crumbs and salted butter. Try serving it with whipped cream.

FOR THE PIECRUST

28 whole Oreo cookies

6 tablespoons salted
   butter, melted

FOR THE FILLING

1 (13½-ounce) can
   coconut milk

¼ cup sugar

½ cup water

5 tablespoons cornstarch

1. **TO MAKE THE PIECRUST:** In a food processor, combine the Oreo cookies and butter and lightly pulse until the mixture is reduced to fine crumbs.

2. Transfer the cookie mixture to a 9- or 10-inch pie pan, making sure the cookie crumbs are spread evenly. Using a spatula, press down firmly to make a well-packed piecrust. Place in the refrigerator and chill for at least 40 minutes.

3. **TO MAKE THE FILLING:** In a pot over medium-high heat, heat the coconut milk and sugar. Bring to a simmer and melt the sugar.

4. In a small bowl, mix the water and cornstarch well. Add the cornstarch slurry to the pot. Simmer for about 3 minutes, until the filling starts to thicken.

5. Pour the filling mixture into the piecrust and place in the refrigerator until it sets, about 2 hours.

6. Slice and serve.

Ingredient Smarts: Make sure that your cornstarch slurry is mixed well so there are no lumps in your haupia. It is important for the custard to be smooth so it is silky once set.

PRUNE MUI

ONE-POT

Prep time: 15 minutes, plus 1 week to soak / **Cook time:** 10 minutes
Makes 1 gallon or 4 (1-quart) mason jars

If you grew up in Hawai'i and hear the words "prune mui," your mouth immediately starts watering. Prune Mui is a sweet and salty unique Hawaiian fruit snack with Chinese roots. If you don't receive a mason jar of homemade Prune Mui for Christmas, then you really are missing out on something special! Here's my version of this classic.

4½ cups firmly packed brown sugar

Juice of 5 lemons (1½ cups)

½ cup dried lemon peel, chopped

2 tablespoons salt

3 tablespoons whiskey or brandy

6 pieces candied ginger, diced

14 whole cloves

1 teaspoon Chinese five-spice powder

1½ pounds dried seedless prunes

1½ pounds dried seedless apricots

1 pound dried mango

1 pound dried cherries

4 ounces dried red seedless li hing mui

1. In a pot, mix the brown sugar, lemon juice, lemon peel, salt, whiskey, candied ginger, cloves, and five-spice powder.

2. Mix well and bring to a simmer over medium-high heat. Once the sugar is melted, remove from the heat and allow the mixture to cool for about 5 minutes.

3. Add the prunes, apricots, mango, cherries, and li hing mui and stir to coat evenly.

4. Tightly pack the mixture into cleaned mason jars and evenly disperse the remaining liquid.

5. Allow to fully cool before covering.

6. Store in a cool, dry, dark place for at least 1 week, shaking and rotating the jars daily for the first week so the fruit stays hydrated.

7. Store in an airtight container in refrigerator for up to 1 month

Ingredient Smarts: *Li hing mui* is an old Chinese specialty that can be found online. The most popular brand is Asian Trans. In order to obtain the most flavor, you must shake the jars daily for at least a week, as this will help the flavor disperse evenly throughout the fruit.

HAWAIIAN CRUMBLE

Prep time: 5 minutes, plus 30 minutes to rest / **Cook time:** 40 minutes / **Serves 6**

I call this "Hawaiian Betty," and it is my take on the popular dish known as Brown Betty, which is like a cobbler. In this recipe, fresh pineapple and coconut caramel sauce with a brown sugar crumble pair perfectly with vanilla ice cream. Tart pineapple balances out the creamy caramel.

FOR THE FILLING

2 cups brown sugar

1 cup heavy (whipping) cream

1 pineapple, cored and cut into ½-inch chunks

1 (20-ounce) can apple pie filling, chopped

FOR THE CRUMBLE

1½ cups all-purpose flour

¾ cup brown sugar

⅓ cup granulated white sugar

½ teaspoon ground cinnamon

Pinch salt

¾ cup (1½ sticks) cold butter

4 tablespoons chopped toasted macadamia nuts*

Vanilla ice cream, for serving

Ingredient Smarts:
Be sure to keep the butter cold and cut it into small cubes to get your crumble perfect.

1. Preheat the oven to 375°F.

2. **TO MAKE THE FILLING:** In a saucepan over medium heat, heat the brown sugar and cream and bring to a simmer. Simmer for 2 minutes, turn off the heat, and set aside.

3. In a large sauté pan or skillet, combine the pineapple and apple filling and cook over medium-high heat for about 5 minutes, until some of the liquid has evaporated. Add the sugar and cream mixture to the fruit and cook for about 5 minutes, until thickened.

4. **TO MAKE THE CRUMBLE:** Meanwhile, in a bowl, mix the flour, brown and white sugars, cinnamon, and salt. Cut the butter into little cubes and gently squeeze it into the flour mixture with your fingers until it turns into a sand-like consistency. Refrigerate for at least 30 minutes before using.

5. Ladle the caramel and fruit mixture into oven-proof ramekins. Top with the crumble.

6. Bake for about 30 minutes, until the crumble is golden and the caramel is bubbling.

7. Serve with toasted macadamia nuts and a scoop of vanilla ice cream.

*Try This:** You can use any toasted chopped nut of your choice.

BANANA CREAM PARFAIT

5-INGREDIENT

Prep time: 10 minutes, plus 3 hours to chill / **Cook time:** 20 minutes / **Serves 4**

Growing up, my grandma and papa had a banana farm. During the summers, I would work at the farm and go with my grandma to the farmers' market to sell the bananas. It's no wonder that I now love bananas, especially the sweet little apple bananas we have here in Hawai'i.

1 (14-ounce) can sweetened condensed milk

1½ cups very cold water

1 (5.1-ounce) box vanilla instant pudding

3 cups heavy (whipping) cream

1 (16-ounce) box gingersnap cookies, crushed*

4 cups diagonally cut ripe bananas

1. In a medium bowl, mix the condensed milk and water until well combined. Add the instant pudding and mix well. Cover and refrigerate for 3 hours.

2. In another bowl, whip the heavy (whipping) cream using a whisk until thickened. Using a rubber spatula, gently fold the whipped cream into the pudding mixture, adding about a quarter at a time, from the outside to the center.

3. In individual mason jars or one large glass bowl add a layer of the ginger-snap cookie crumbs. Add a layer of ripe bananas on top of the cookie crumbs. Top with a layer of the pudding-cream mixture. Repeat the layering process until the jars are full.

*__Try This:__ Substitute graham crackers or Oreos instead of gingersnap cookies to create different versions of this delicious dish.

FURIKAKE PARTY MIX

Prep time: 10 minutes / **Cook time:** 1 hour / **Serves 4**

This crunchy treat started out as a holiday favorite that turned into a monthly snack. Every Christmas my mom would make multiple batches of this homemade party mix to give away, and we would spend a whole week eating it. I decided that I didn't have to have an excuse to enjoy this year-round.

1 pound butter, melted

1 tablespoon furikake

1 cup sugar

2 tablespoons Worcestershire sauce

1 teaspoon garlic powder

3 dashes Tabasco sauce

1 (12-ounce) box Rice Chex

1 (14-ounce) bag Bugles

1 (16-ounce) box Honeycomb cereal

2 cups stick pretzels

2 cups honey roasted peanuts

2 cups toasted whole macadamia nuts

1. Preheat the oven to 250°F.

2. In a large bowl, combine all the ingredients and toss until very well mixed.

3. Spread the mixture out evenly on a baking sheet. Bake for 1 hour, stirring every 15 minutes.

4. Store in an airtight container for up to 1 week at room temperature.

COCONUT BREAD PUDDING

Prep time: 15 minutes, plus 25 minutes to soak / **Cook time:** 50 minutes / **Serves 4**

Bread pudding is a popular dessert everywhere and comes in many variations. My version uses coconut milk to give it a thicker texture and richer flavor. This is a coconut lover's dessert, and toasted coconut flakes make the perfect garnish for this dish.

FOR THE BREAD PUDDING

2 cups coconut milk

2 tablespoons unsalted butter, plus more for greasing

1 teaspoon vanilla extract

⅓ cup sugar

Pinch salt

½ loaf Portuguese sweet bread, brioche, or challah, cut into 2-inch chunks

3 large eggs, beaten

FOR THE COCONUT CARAMEL SAUCE

1 cup brown sugar

½ cup coconut milk

1. Preheat the oven to 350°F. Grease a 4- to 6-cup baking dish with butter.

2. **TO MAKE THE BREAD PUDDING:** In a saucepan over medium-high heat, heat the coconut milk, butter, vanilla, sugar, and salt. Cook for about 5 minutes, until everything is melted together. Turn off the heat and allow to cool.

3. Fill the baking dish with the bread cubes.

4. Add the eggs to the cooled coconut milk mixture and whisk to incorporate.

5. Pour the coconut milk and egg mixture over the bread and allow to soak for about 25 minutes.

6. Bake for 30 to 45 minutes, or until the custard is set but still has a little movement in the middle.

7. **TO MAKE THE COCONUT CARAMEL SAUCE:** Meanwhile, in a saucepan over medium-high heat, cook the brown sugar and coconut milk down for 5 to 8 minutes, until slightly thickened.

8. Serve the bread pudding with the sauce.

Ingredient Smarts: It's best to use one- to two-day old bread that is dried out so it can absorb the custard like a sponge.

Loco Moco,
PAGE 50, with
Mushroom Onion
Gravy, PAGE 99

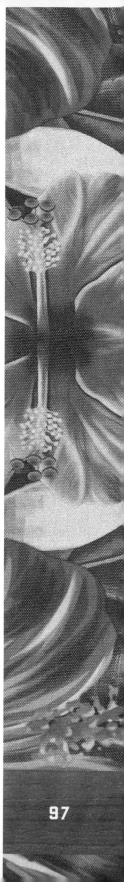

CHAPTER SEVEN

Homemade Staples

CHILI PEPPER WATER

5-INGREDIENT   QUICK

Prep time: 10 minutes, plus 24 hours to age / **Cook time:** 5 minutes / **Makes 4 cups**

This hot sauce is like Tabasco, sriracha, and Cholula all wrapped into one. It is the only hot sauce that I know of that is truly Hawaiian! At my restaurant, we make our chili "peppah" water in five-gallon buckets, and it needs to be made once a week! There are different variations for different cultures. Only water, chiles, limu (seaweed), and Hawaiian salt are needed for the Hawaiian version. This is a Filipino version that adds some garlic and vinegar to the mix.

10 Hawaiian chiles*

1 tablespoon salt

2 cups water

1 cup distilled white vinegar

1 (1-inch) piece fresh ginger

4 garlic cloves, minced

1. In a food processor or blender, combine the chiles and salt and blend.

2. In a medium pot over medium-high heat, combine the water, vinegar, and ginger and bring to a boil.

3. Turn off the heat and stir in the garlic and ground chiles.

4. Pour the mixture into a clean jar and store in refrigerator for at least 24 hours before serving. This will keep in the refrigerator up to 3 weeks.

*Try This: If you can't find Hawaiian chile peppers (which can be very difficult on the mainland), feel free to use Thai birds-eye chile peppers instead.

Ingredient Smarts: If you don't want the chili water to be too hot, you can blend half the chiles and leave the rest whole; for an even milder taste, you can leave all the chiles whole.

MUSHROOM ONION GRAVY

Prep time: 5 minutes / **Cook time:** 20 minutes / **Makes 5 cups**

Brown gravy is crazy popular here. Growing up at my dad's plate lunch restaurant, we had a code for our orders and would put a little "g" over all the items that the customer wanted gravy on, so "ggg" on the order meant gravy on the rice, mac salad, and meat—aka "gravy all over"—and was ordered multiple times a day.

1 tablespoon neutral oil

1 yellow onion, julienned

1 (8-ounce) package
   mushrooms, sliced

4 garlic cloves, minced

4 tablespoons
   unsalted butter

4 tablespoons
   all-purpose flour

4 cups beef stock

2 teaspoons sugar

2 teaspoons salt

1 teaspoon freshly
   ground black pepper

1. In a sauté pan, heat the oil over medium heat. Add the onion and slowly cook for about 10 minutes, until slightly caramelized.

2. Add the mushrooms, garlic, and butter and cook for about 3 minutes, until the butter is melted.

3. Add the flour and mix. Continue to cook over medium heat for about 2 minutes, stirring constantly, until browned.

4. Add the beef stock, sugar, salt, and pepper and bring to a simmer, whisking well to get any clumps out.

5. Simmer for 3 to 5 minutes, until the gravy starts to thicken. Store in an airtight container for up 5 days in the fridge.

Ingredient Smarts: If you want to make it gluten-free or less heavy, use Cornstarch Slurry (page 102) instead of flour.

TEMPURA BATTER

5-INGREDIENT ONE-POT QUICK

Prep time: 5 minutes / **Cook time:** 5 minutes / **Makes 3 cups**

I love the versatility of Tempura Batter. You can make the obvious, like vegetables and seafood. But you can also fry things like avocado and Oreos, fry up some "crunchies" to put on salads and rice, or make one of my favorites: tempura-fried pickles! Try this super simple recipe with confidence.

1 cup all-purpose flour

Pinch salt

½ cup ice

1 cup soda water

1. In a large bowl, combine the flour, salt, and ice.

2. Using a fork, slowly add in the soda water, taking care not to overmix. A few small lumps are okay and recommended (the ice will still be whole but will slowly melt and keep the mixture cold). Use immediately.

Ingredient Smarts: The ice is a key ingredient; keeping the gluten cold will create a crispy, light texture. When trying to tempura-batter something that the batter keeps slipping off of (especially vegetables), try dipping the food in water, flour, then the batter to create the best hold.

BUG JUICE

Prep time: 5 minutes / **Makes 1½ cups**

The name "bug juice" comes from the little bits of black pepper floating around in this extremely versatile salty, sour dip. When I was a little kid, we would get tangerines from the yard of the old lady who lived next door and would dip them in Bug Juice for one of my absolute favorite summer snacks! This sauce is a delicious fat-free salad dressing replacement, great for dipping your oranges or tangerines in, drizzling some seared or grilled fish, or serving with sashimi or some fresh avocado.

½ cup soy sauce*

½ cup distilled
white vinegar

4 tablespoons water

Juice of 1 lemon

1 tablespoon sugar

2 teaspoons freshly
ground black pepper

In a bowl, combine the soy sauce, vinegar, water, lemon juice, sugar, and pepper and enjoy. Store in an airtight container in the refrigerator for up to 3 weeks.

*Try This: If not using Aloha brand soy sauce, add 1 more tablespoon of water.

CORNSTARCH SLURRY

5-INGREDIENT QUICK

Prep time: 1 minute / **Makes 1½ cups**

A cornstarch slurry is as crucial to a Hawaiian kitchen as a roux would be in Southern cuisine. We use this to thicken everything, as well as for breading and in our marinades. I remember there was always a washed-out oyster sauce can filled with a cornstarch slurry next to the wok station, ready to thicken any sauce at my dad's Hawaiian restaurant. Keeping a little cornstarch nearby will go a long way for many dishes in this book.

½ cup cornstarch

1 cup water or cold liquid

1. **TO MAKE THE SLURRY:** In a bowl, using your index and middle finger, mix the cornstarch and water. This can sit for a while, but make sure to mix it before using.

2. **TO USE THE SLURRY:** Make sure that the liquid you are using is at a boil, as cornstarch is a heat-activated thickener.

3. With a whisk in one hand and the slurry in the other, slowly add the slurry while whisking continuously.

4. Add a little at a time; it will thicken instantly, so you can gauge the thickness that you want.

5. When you get your desired thickness, turn down the heat and simmer for about 3 minutes to cook off any cornstarch taste. Keep in mind that when this sauce gets cool, it will get even thicker. Heating it up will bring it right back to the consistency it was when you first thickened it.

Ingredient Smarts: Cornstarch slurry can last a few days on the counter, but it will separate within hours. When that happens use your pointer finger and mix; the cornstarch will be very hard, but it will soften up quickly once you mix it.

GARLIC-CHILI OIL CRUNCH

QUICK

Prep time: 5 minutes, plus overnight to chill / **Cook time:** 5 minutes / **Makes 4 cups**

This recipe certainly is a mix of cultures, as you find chili oils in not only a lot of Asian cuisines but also European recipes. This is the chunky, spicy, delicious stuff you find in the condiment section, that adds so much flavor to whatever it is that you add a dollop. It is also perfect when mixed into butter and smothered on a steak or on the delicious Grilled Teriyaki Tofu (page 76).

½ cup dried red chili flakes*

¼ cup dried fried shallots or dried minced onions

3 tablespoons dried fried garlic*

4 whole star anise

2 cardamom pods

3 tablespoons chopped fresh ginger

2 tablespoons sugar

1 tablespoon salt

1 tablespoon soy sauce

1 teaspoon ground Szechuan peppercorns (optional)

10 garlic cloves, thinly sliced

3½ cups neutral oil

1. In a large heatproof bowl, combine the chili flakes, shallots, fried garlic, star anise, cardamom pods, ginger, sugar, salt, soy sauce, and peppercorns (if using). Set aside.

2. In a medium saucepan over medium heat, combine the garlic and oil and slowly heat for 3 to 5 minutes, until the garlic is golden.

3. Pour the warm garlic oil over the chili mixture and mix until well combined.

4. Pour the chili crunch into a glass jar or bowl and let sit in the refrigerator overnight before serving. Store, covered, for up to 2 months in the refrigerator.

*Try This: Use your favorite dried chili flakes, or you can get whole dried chiles and grind them in a food processor, using a colander to separate some of the seeds out. Dried fried garlic is available online.

KOREAN BARBECUE SAUCE

ONE-POT QUICK

Prep time: 5 minutes / **Cook time:** 5 minutes / **Makes 3 cups**

Korean Barbecue Sauce is very similar to Teriyaki Sauce (page 105) with a few key differences. Toasted sesame seeds, sesame oil, and scallions help give it a distinct flavor to its relative. This is great with kalbi ribs, and a thickened version of this makes amazing Korean chicken wings.

1 cup water

1 cup sugar

1 cup soy sauce

2 tablespoons minced garlic

1 tablespoon minced fresh ginger

1 tablespoon toasted sesame seeds

1 tablespoon sesame oil

1 tablespoon sambal oelek

1. In a saucepan or small pot over high heat, bring the water to a boil.

2. Add the sugar and stir until dissolved.

3. Turn to a low simmer and add the soy sauce, garlic, ginger, sesame seeds, sesame oil, and sambal oelek.

4. Cook for 2 more minutes. Store in an airtight container for up to 2 weeks in the refrigerator.

Ingredient Smarts: If you like more spice, add as much sambal oelek as you like!

TERIYAKI SAUCE

5-INGREDIENT ONE-POT QUICK

Prep time: 5 minutes / **Cook time:** 5 minutes / **Makes 3 cups**

Teriyaki Sauce is probably the most common staple in Hawaiian cooking. Every Hawaiian restaurant will have some form of teriyaki, whether it's teriyaki chicken, beef, or pork. This sauce truly is a representation of plate lunch as it combines different flavors and cultures to create a version unique to the islands. Thickening this sauce (with Cornstarch Slurry, page 102) creates a glaze that is amazing on just about anything.

1 cup soy sauce

1 cup water

1 cup sugar

1 tablespoon minced garlic

1 tablespoon minced
   fresh ginger

1. In a saucepan over low heat, combine the soy sauce, water, and sugar and slowly cook until the sugar just dissolves.

2. Remove from the heat immediately and add the garlic and ginger.

3. Store in an airtight container in the refrigerator for up to 2 weeks.

Ingredient Smarts: You don't want to boil this whole sauce, since boiling water can ruin the flavors of fresh ginger and garlic.

KATSU SAUCE

5-INGREDIENT   ONE-POT   QUICK

Prep time: 5 minutes / **Makes 1½ cups**

I specifically refrain from calling this "Chicken" Katsu Sauce because this sauce is not just for chicken. Katsu can be pork, chicken, fish, and I have even seen Spam katsu! This sauce has a sweet tang that brings huge amounts of flavor to just about anything.

½ cup ketchup

4 tablespoons Worcestershire sauce

2 tablespoons oyster sauce

1 tablespoon brown sugar

Freshly ground black pepper

In a bowl, mix the ketchup, Worcestershire sauce, oyster sauce, brown sugar, and pepper and enjoy. Store in an airtight container in the refrigerator for 2 weeks.

Musubi
PAGE 27

MEASUREMENT CONVERSIONS

VOLUME EQUIVALENTS	U.S. STANDARD	U.S. STANDARD (OUNCES)	METRIC (APPROXIMATE)
LIQUID	2 tablespoons	1 fl. oz.	30 mL
	¼ cup	2 fl. oz.	60 mL
	½ cup	4 fl. oz.	120 mL
	1 cup	8 fl. oz.	240 mL
	1½ cups	12 fl. oz.	355 mL
	2 cups or 1 pint	16 fl. oz.	475 mL
	4 cups or 1 quart	32 fl. oz.	1 L
	1 gallon	128 fl. oz.	4 L
DRY	⅛ teaspoon	—	0.5 mL
	¼ teaspoon	—	1 mL
	½ teaspoon	—	2 mL
	¾ teaspoon	—	4 mL
	1 teaspoon	—	5 mL
	1 tablespoon	—	15 mL
	¼ cup	—	59 mL
	⅓ cup	—	79 mL
	½ cup	—	118 mL
	⅔ cup	—	156 mL
	¾ cup	—	177 mL
	1 cup	—	235 mL
	2 cups or 1 pint	—	475 mL
	3 cups	—	700 mL
	4 cups or 1 quart	—	1 L
	½ gallon	—	2 L
	1 gallon	—	4 L

OVEN TEMPERATURES

FAHRENHEIT	CELSIUS (APPROXIMATE)
250°F	120°C
300°F	150°C
325°F	165°C
350°F	180°C
375°F	190°C
400°F	200°C
425°F	220°C
450°F	230°C

WEIGHT EQUIVALENTS

U.S. STANDARD	METRIC (APPROXIMATE)
½ ounce	15 g
1 ounce	30 g
2 ounces	60 g
4 ounces	115 g
8 ounces	225 g
12 ounces	340 g
16 ounces or 1 pound	455 g

REFERENCE

Fox, Catherine Toth. "Hawaii's Rainbow of Cultures and How They Got to the Islands." *Hawai'i Magazine*, September 26, 2017. HawaiiMagazine.com/Hawaiis-rainbow-of-cultures-and-how-they-got-to-the-islands.

INDEX

ACKNOWLEDGMENTS

I am blessed to have had a solid foundation from my parents, who have shown me how hard work and determination always pays off. Without all their sacrifices and everything that they have done for me and my brothers, I would not be the man and chef I am today. I also want to thank my amazing wife and life partner, who has been the key to everything I have done in the last 14 years. I can say without a doubt, I would not be where I am without her. Finally, I want to say thank you to my three girls, Olive, Grace, and Poppy, for showing me the meaning of life and what is important.

ABOUT THE AUTHOR

Chef Philip "Ippy" Aiona was born and raised on the Big Island of Hawai'i. His father is a native Hawaiian who owned a Hawaiian plate lunch restaurant for many years. His Italian American mom, who owned and operated an Italian restaurant on the Big Island, is from New York. Chef Ippy grew up working at both his parents' restaurants. After graduating high school, he attended the California Culinary Academy, Le Cordon Bleu, where he met his wife, Genna. Chef Ippy was a finalist on Food Network's *Food Network Star* and has been listed on the *Forbes* "30 under 30 Food and Wine" list twice. He currently owns Ippy's Hawaiian BBQ and The Dizzy Pita in his hometown of Waimea on the Big Island with his wife and daughters.